SOUTHERN AFRICAN

SOTHO NAMES

FOR BABIES

I0415240

DIMAKATSO MALEKA-KARAS

SOUTHERN AFRICAN

SOTHO NAMES

FOR BABIES

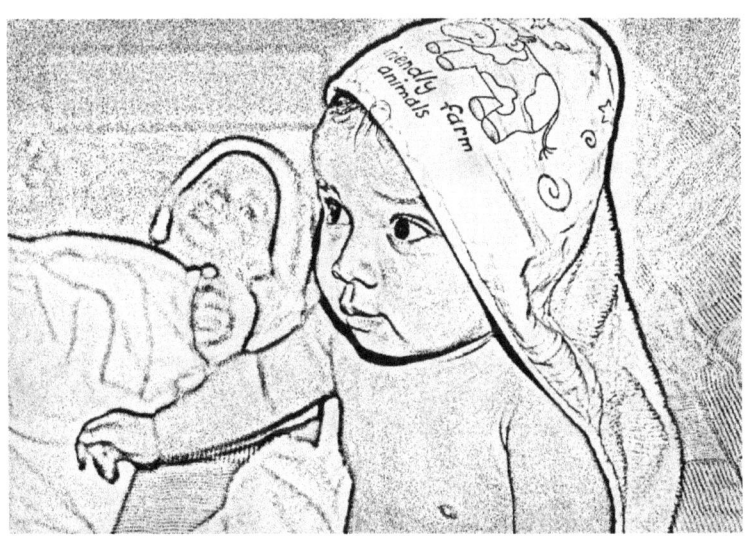

DIMAKATSO MALEKA-KARAS

FOR MY CHILDREN

AKAMIYA, PABALLO, KHUMO AND DIKETSO

THIS IS TO REMIND YOU AND GENERATIONS TO COME
OF YOUR

AFRICAN ROOTS

CONTENTS

"BITSO LEBE KE SEROMO"

"A BAD NAME IS ILL-OMENED"

ACKNOWLEDGEMENTS

A massive 'thanks' to all those who have contributed to this book in any form or shape especially those who spoke sePedi, seSotho and Setswana to me.

Great thanks to my friends Sam Phalafala and Duke Mosupye for supplying me with lists of names to start me off. You're both very special to me.

To Lilly Maepa, my best friend in the entire world, you're just too old for your age and I say that with a big smile. Thanks for your support, advice, incredible knowledge of idioms and for being my person.

To Andreas Karas, for your belief in this book, endless support and for finding invaluable reference books when I thought I couldn't find anymore sources for translations. I sometimes felt like you wanted to write the book. Your knowledge of Afrikaans came in handy.

To papa, Mr David Maleka; thanks for making me fall in love with this beautiful language of ours, for teaching us Pedi idioms and for being my reference book.

My Tswana grandmother, koko Mmane (Mashikoane Matjila), I love you dearly. Thank you for stepping in and never complaining nor tiring of my phone

1

calls with requests for translations, explanations and tales. I'm in awe of your memory and state of mind.

Mary Judge, your children's Irish names planted a desire within me to know more about our African names and to appreciate their uniqueness. Thank you for this inspiration.

My big sister Freda Maleka, thank you for your endless support; the painting made an amazing cover.

My sister-in-law Lerato, my brother Tebogo, Keagile and Obakeng for patiently waiting for the book - the wait is now over. I used stories from your lives to help with translations as well as the introduction. I love you all.

John Firth, thank you for editing my work – your knowledge on the subject is amazing; you're definitely in the right field. First of many more to come, I hope.

Leago Sebesho my darling girl, you came to visit and I gave you a manuscript to read. You read, corrected and made suggestions while keeping a smile on your face. Really appreciated!

My friends KG, Dina, Pat, Sesupo, Elsie Malebo and Ntombi – thank you all for being part of my life.

This book took 5 years to complete which really felt like an eternity but worth the time invested. Thank you all.

PRONUNCIATION

Most languages (French, German, Greek, Spanish, Russian, etc.) but English, have sounds that are similar to those used in the Sotho language. The list below includes 31 consonants and seven vowels to help with pronunciation.

Vowels

a   as in art, ask e.g **Aba** (to share)

e   as in **see**, **bee** e.g Tsebo (knowledge)

ê   as in send, an ant e.g Metsi (water)

i   as in **ink**, **link** e.g Bitso (name)

o   as in the **soon**, **moon** e.g Monna (a gentleman)

ô   as in **lock**, **dock**, **mock** e.g Maboko (poems)

u   as in **bull**, **kudu**, **kumquat** e.g bula (open)

3

Consonants

b   as in **b**owl e.g. **b**ana (children), **b**atho (people)

bj   as in **bi**en (French), **Bj**örk (Icelandic) e.g. **bj**alo (as it is), **bj**ana (child-like)

c   as in tweep but with an **s** i.e **tswee**p e.g. lencoe (the word) pronounced Lent*swe*

d   as in dark, **d**ean e.g. **d**iketso (deeds), **d**ineo (gifts), **d**itshego (laughter)

f   as in **f**ace, **f**all e.g. **f**eta (pass), **f**etsa (finish)

g   as in the **ja**mon (Spanish) e.g. **g**ata (to step on), **g**angwe (once)

h   as in **h**otel, **h**ard e.g. **h**anang (refuse), **h**eso (home)

hl   as in **Chl**oe e.g. **hl**ano (the number five), **hl**ompho (respect)

j   as in **j**am, **J**anuary e.g. e**j**a (eat), **j**ase (jacket)

k   as in **k**appa (greek letter), **C**ote d'Ivoire e.g. **k**atse (cat), **k**otse (danger)

kg   as in **cr**oss, **cr**y, **kr**one (Norwegian currency) but rougher e.g. **kg**osi (king)

kh   as in **Kh**an, **Kh**mer Rouge e.g. **Kh**umo (wealth)

l   as in **l**amb, **l**and e.g. **l**etla (wait), **l**eka (try)

m   as in **m**other e.g. **m**ma (mother)

n   as in **n**ap, **n**eck e.g. **n**eo (gift), **n**alata (needle)

ny   as in **ne**o**n** Putting no and yes together (nyes)

ng   as in cry**ing**, talk**ing** e.g. **ng**apa (scratch), **ng**ata (many)

nq   sound made when the tongue is flat and pushing on palate e.g. **nq**ae (sorry)

p   as in **p**ace, **p**en e.g. **p**elo (heart), **p**ala (pole)

ph   as in **p**ark, **p**ast e.g. **ph**ahla (a gap), **ph**eto (conclusion)

q   an ô sound made with toungue rolled on palate e.g. mo**q**o**q**o (conversation)

r	as in run e.g. rata (like), rra (father), rona (we)
s	as in sail, sit e.g. sala (stay), sello (a cry)
sh	as in shame e.g. shitwa (hinders), mashemo (the ploughing fields)
t	as in stammer, stand e.g. teko (a test, challenge), teballo (forgiveness)
tj	**as in Tchaikovsky (Russian composer)** e.g. tjale (shawl)
tl	as in clean, close e.g. tlalo (full; fulfilment), matla (strength, power)
tlh	as in closet, clothe e.g. tlholo (victory), tlhompho (respect)
ts	as in tsar (Russian), tsunami (Japanes) e.g tsie (locust), tseno (entrance)
w	as in walk, want e.g. warona (ours)
y	as in yes e.g. yena (that one), ya bona (theirs)

ABBREVIATIONS

adj   adjective

b   boy(s)

dim   diminutive

g   girl(s)

pl   plural (also used courteously when addressing adults or anyone older)

s   singular

v   verb(s)

INTRODUCTION

"What's in a name ...?" Juliet asks of Romeo [*Romeo and Juliet: II, ii,* 43] declaring that a name is a meaningless notion. In their struggle yes, it may be meaningless but when naming a child, the name becomes everything. A name can either make or break the person; it can also invite torment and ridicule; but if well chosen, it may command respect, fear or admiration. A name defines who one is and who one can ultimately become. Yes, there's definitely something to a name!

Naming of a child in any culture has always been a delicate subject. It can be very easy for others to choose a name but in most instances, this tends to be very lengthy (sometimes even long after the child has been born) as parents ponder over names trying to find the one that 'speaks to them'. Why do parents from various cultural backgrounds choose particular names for their children? Why then do certain names become more popular than others? Could the naming process be merely a fashionable stunt or just based on familiarity or familial connotations? In this book, an attempt has been made to explain the processes, beliefs and trends involved in the naming of a child in some African cultures of South Africa.

South Africa isn't called the Rainbow nation for nothing; it's a multicultural society boasting eleven official languages some of which are riddled with many tribal dialects. This book however, covers only the names used by Sotho-speaking people. Sotho or seSotho as is known, encompasses three very distinct yet fundamentally intelligible languages which are: seTswana (Tswana; seKgatla), sePedi (northern Sotho) and seShweshwe (south Sotho or seSotho sa Borwa). SeTswana is spoken mainly in Botswana through to the West of South Africa (North-West province) and down in the Northern Cape. Sepedi or Northern Sotho has many dialects and is spoken mostly in areas found in the Northern Limpopo region. Southern Sotho (or Sesotho), is the language of the Free State, Lesotho (the kingdom of Basotho) and the North-Eastern parts of the Eastern Cape. Although these languages are still considered as three separate languages for political and historical reasons, they are very similar with shared beliefs and customs.

Like many cultures, seSotho is dominated and shaped by ancient yet significant beliefs, myths, legends and proverbs. An old Sotho proverb which states *"Bitso lebe ke seromo"* literally meaning "a bad name is ill-omened" gets parents thinking and has in turn, made the naming process significant. Indeed, the given name will not only serve as an identity but can have bearing on the type of person the individual will grow up to be. Most southern African names are an interpretation of some sort of historical event, often describing various individual (e.g one's state of mind), familial or group social experiences.

Death, especially of children, plays a vital part in the naming process as well as failure of a bride to conceive or deliver live offspring (still births), pregnancy out of wedlock, sudden familial wealth or success, famine, drought and even abundance. Basically, whatever the circumstances prior to the birth of a particular child are taken into consideration and can dictate the name to be chosen. Names can also represent social norms and values, status roles or authority (tribes, clan, respectable heads, kingship organized by lineage) as well as personality (e.g child crying incessantly or just sleeping peacefully) and individual attributes (such as dark or light skin tone, beauty, large headed, or friendly face).

Trends have now changed. People now tend to choose names because they just like the name, how it sounds or just its uniqueness, forgetting or even unaware that the very name chosen may have had some historical meaning. Others prefer to use surnames, especially when naming the child after someone who's touched their lives in a positive way. Others simply use names of food or objects that had an impact during their upbringing. It is also still very acceptable to name children after their grandparents or relatives in order to perpetuate the names of ancestors. Grandparents often expect this gesture as a form of recognition for their contribution in the upbringing of the parent. In other instances, if the relation's name is found to be too old-fashioned or nowadays sounds awful, the child would get a second name by which it will be known and use the other as a middle name.

BaSotho also believe that children are a gift from *Modimo* God, the Great Almighty. They believe too in *Badimo,* the ancestral spirits perceived to be agents of God [*Badimo* being the plural of *Modimo* - God]. *Badimo* can also refer to family members who have passed on and are supposed to protect those left behind. Likewise, the belief that stars represent family members who have passed on was widespread in Europe and North America. *Badimo* are revered to a point that celebrations are often held in their honour, especially when things aren't going so well for certain family members. Thus, baSotho (or other African groups) believe that one shouldn't anger *Badimo* for fear of what would befall those members. Circumstances such as barrenness, miscarriages, difficulty in conceiving, divorces, loss of jobs, can be and are therefore attributed as disfavour of *Modimo* or *Badimo* the ancestors.

After such misfortunes, celebratory names like *Tebogo* (thanks), *Thabo* (happiness) and *Tumelo* (belief) are often used. Names of this kind are also used when or if a child of a preferred gender is finally born. Birth of twins is also regarded as a special gift and blessing from the ancestors and the naming can reflect this emotion. Formerly, twins were given the same name with the twin delivered last being given the diminutive form of the first-born's name e.g. *Thabo* (first twin) and *Thabonyana* (small Thabo, second); *Mpho* and *Mphonyana*; *Mashiko* and *Mashikoana*. If blessed with a boy and a girl twin, names such as *Thabo* (boy) and *Thabang* (girl) or *Tshepo* (boy) and *Tshepiso* (girl) -among many- are used but other non-matching or non-sequential names have recently been widely used.

The naming process continues even in matrimony. By tradition, the in-laws should give the bride a marital name (bridal name) by which the husband is also expected to call her. This part of tradition is still observed even today by the younger generation who excitedly anticipate the children with whom they will be blessed. Traditionally, the marital name should incorporate the name that the in-laws expect or wish the daughter-in-law to give to her first child (e.g. *Mmakeneiloe*: **Mma/Ma** – mother and **Keneiloe** – child's name i.e. mother of Keneiloe), even though she had another name in mind. Often, the child will have a second name chosen by the mother which coincides with or reflects her state of well-being at birth. Mostly, the second names are given to honour the bride's parents to show appreciation and to enforce some representation of her side of the family. In most cases, the name will reflect the way the bride (*makoti*) is or was treated by her in-laws prior to the event, thus resulting in names such as perseverance (*Boitshoko*) and hardship (*Tshwenyo*) among others. These names are normally given out of spite but can have dire results for the child.

With other Sotho tribes, naming of a bride is harsher and may only be done once she has produced a child. When the prefix *Mma* (see above) is affixed to a name it simply means 'mother of so and so' and when *Ra* is affixed, it means 'father of so and so'. To confuse matters, *Bapedi* (northern Sothos) sometimes formulate girls' names by attaching the prefix *Ra* to nouns or verbs, or to the name of a maternal uncle after whom she is to be named. If the maternal uncle's name is *Madimetja* then the girl's name will be **Ra**madimetja sounding male but acceptable as a female name. Out of respect *tlhompho*, adults are never referred to by their names but instead as mother or father of so and so. Children, especially, often use the first child's name after *Mma/mama* or *Rra/papa/ntate* (e.g *mamaTshidi*, mother of *Tshidi*) to address grown-ups.

Direto (*Sereto* in the singular) -known as Praise Names/Poems- are still used but sadly less and less, to a point where the young may never have heard of such. These are grouped under *Digagabi* (reptiles), *Dinonyane* (birds), *Diphoofolo/Diphôlôgôlô* (animals) and *metlhare* (trees or plants) and are meant to portray admirable qualities like strength, skilfulness, intelligence and some physical attributes. *Direto* are also given to boy initiates (*Makolwane*) where the tradition is still followed. The kings and chiefs (*Marena*), and warriors (*Batlhabane*) of yesteryear, as well as leaders and presidents, are also honoured in naming processes. At family gatherings like weddings and funerals people do tend to ask what one's *Sereto* is and often -mainly among the older generation– one will be able to recite one's praise poems. Unfortunately, *Direto* are often unknown to the younger generations and are slowly becoming a forgotten part of the naming processes.

Names will always remain a personal choice but hopefully this book will enable parents, especially of generations to come, to choose names for their children and to keep our history alive. Names, variants and meanings have been given where possible. Some names have been freely invented or created by joining words together to make new ones, making them difficult to translate; but an attempt has been made and hopefully with minimal errors. This book holds a comprehensive selection of names and is designed to help parents in making a choice. I also hope that it will help my children, grandchildren and generations to come, to keep using these beautiful Sotho names we have. Enjoy!

Dimakatso Maleka-Karas (2012)

GENDER-FREE NAMES
(UNISEX)

A

Abago

Absence; they (plural out of respect) are absent - often when father is not around

Abelang

Share, divide up, allocate, assign

Abueng

Verbalise, utter, exclaim; speak about it

Afuwa (Afua)

Given, has been bequethed

Aganang / Agang

Aga (v) – to build; build together, develop, shape or help each other prosper

Agisegang

Develop, grow together. Let you/the family grow and develop.

Akanyang

Be thoughtful, considerate; think!

Alima (A*d*ima)

Borrow

Ama

Get involved, be part of

Amogelang

Receive, Accept

Araba

Answer, respond

Arabang (*pl*)

Answer, respond

Arabelo

Response, receptive, responsive

Arabelang

Answer, respond, to

Ata

Multiply, increase

Atang (*pl*)

Multiply; grow as a family

Atiso

Multiply; increase, grow as a family

Atlegang

Prosper, thrive, succeed; flourish

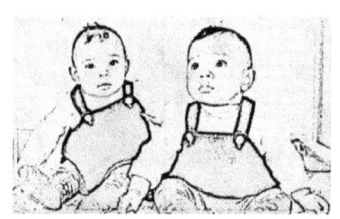

B

Baatseba (Batseba)

Ba – they; also used as a plural out of respect for the elders (he/she). They... know, are informed, are aware or are enlightened

Baete (Baet*i*)

Guests, visitors

Bafedile

They've been obliterated (*finished or died off*). Also means conclusion; they're done especially if last child; completion

Bahlolegile

Hlola – to defeat; they've been defeated, they've succumbed

Bakang

Praise (the Lord)

Bakgethwa

Kgethwa (adj) – holy; the holy ones; saints

Kgetha (v) – to choose; the chosen ones

Banthata

I am loved; they love me

Baphelile (Baphe*di*le)

They've lived (health of offspring); experienced (knowledgeable)

Baratang

Rata – to love, wish or desire; those who love, desire or wish; choice

Barekgona

Kgona – able to handle
They [**Ba**] can handle us;
they know how to deal
with us

Bareng

What do they say; talk,
gossip

Barileng

What have they said?

Basedi

Of light; enlightened

Bodule

Of character: suttle,
almost boring.

Dula – live/exist (in a
place): abode, dwelling

Bogakeng

(In) bravery - a brave
person; aggressive and
confrontational

Bohlale (Bo*tlh*ale)

Wisdom; insight

Bohlokwa

Important; significant

Bohloeki

Pure; purity

Boikanyo

Rely upon, trusted

Bokamoso

The future, prospect

Bokang

Praise, adore, worship,
commend

Bonang

Bona (v) – to see; see or witness, this

Bongoe (Bongwe)

One, alone

Bophelo / Botshelo

Life, living, existence

Botang

Glorify, worship (the Lord); trust

Botho

Humanity; humane, considerate

Botshele

Daybreak, new beginnings

Busang

Reign, govern; return

C

Choarelo (*Tsh*warelo)

Forgiveness

Choaro (*Tsh*waro)

An assembly; to hold; to apprehend

Chuene (*Tsh*wene)

Monkey; a vervet monkey

Chuma (*Tsh*uma)

Alight, ablaze

D

Diatile (Liatile)

They've multiplied,
increased

Dibe (Libe)

Sins; of which is ...

Dibeng

In/of sin, sinful

Diboko

Praises, rejoice

Diemo

Honourable, high calibre,
importance, of high
standing; a stand point

Dieto

Journeys

Difuro

Furrows

Dihlodi

A plant – Mung bean
(*Phaseolus aureus*)

Dikgaogelo

Di (pl) countless or
endless mercy;
compassion, leniency;

Dikhutso

Peace, silence; rest,
tranquillity

Dikopano

Kopano - unity (several);
meetings, congregations

Dimakatso

A marvel, surprises

Dinthwele

That which has carried, helped one usually in hardship; supportive; that which eases my pain or hardship

Ditebogo

Thanks, gratefulness

Dithabo

Countless joys

Dithomo

Beginnings, foundations (s - Thomo)

Dithoriso

Rorisa (v) – worship; multiple worships

Ditshego

Tshega – to laugh, giggle. Much laughter, giggles; happiness, joy (s – setshego – laughter from an individual)

Ditshepo

Hopes (s – Tshepo)

Ditshele

Qualms, quarrels, complaints, objection

Ditshela

Tshela (v) – to cross, abridge. Have overstepped, crossed to safety; child number six tshela

Dumetse

Believed; accepted

E

Ebang

Just be ... (delighted, strong?)

Efua (Efuwa)

T'is given, bequeathed upon

Elelwang

Be aware, informed; take notice

Eletsang

Advise ... (them), consult, guide

Emameleng

Listen, pay attention; listen up

Emang

Wait (for); stand up (and be counted)

Esi

One, alone

Etang

Visit (pay a visit), call upon

Etsane (Etsang)

Etsa (v) – to do; A doer - One who makes things happen; an achiever, go-getter

Ewetse

Go wa – to fall; it has fallen ...

F

Fatang

Dig deeper (as an
encouragement)

Fenyang

Be victorious; unbeaten,
win

Fue (Fuwe)

Given, bequeathed or
bestowed upon

G

Gaosi

Nosi (Osi) – alone (adj);
He/she is <u>not</u> alone

Gaoretelelwe

'No one turns their back
on you'; command
respect

Gaositwe

Sitwa – hinder; you're
<u>not</u> hindered,
incompetent, inhibited.
One who is very
competent, capable; also
powerful

Garaipha

Ipha – to give oneself;
we (the family) have not
bequeathed, given,
bestowed this gift
(baby?) upon us i.e God
has given us

Gasebolelwe

Bolela – to talk; that which is not or cannot be spoken of; it's hush-hush, secretive

Gaitsewe

Itsi – to know; it's unknown, mysterious, unfamiliar, secret [*often if father is unknown*]

Goitseone

Only He (God) knows

Gomolang

Quieten, calm down; be consoled

Gomolemo

Merciful, gracious; God is merciful. Also – Ti's better if … (that way).

Gomotsegang

Be consoled, comforted

Gontse

It's as it should be. All is fine, acceptable; that's enough (reprimand)

Gopolang

Remember, reminisce, evoke

Gorata

To love or be loved; liked

Gotsebamang

Tsebo – knowledge; 'Who knows?' Only He (God) knows

H

Halekopane

Kopano – unity; there's no unity, togetherness or sense of unity; lack of neighbourliness

Halerekoe (Halerekwe)

Reka – to purchase; that which cannot be bought – very precious; signifies strong character

Hlabane

Hlaba – to stab, pierce; War, battle - the one who battles or is in battle. Also a town in the North-West Province

Hlalefang

Be or show intelligence; wisdom

Hlakiso

Abuse, mistreatment; poverty

Hlakisong

Where one is ill-treated or there's a lot suffering [*often when in-laws are unkind to the daughter-in-law*]; a place of poverty especially while mother was expectant

Hlatlane

Hlatla – to follow, succeed another. A follower - one who follows quite soon after the first especially with first two siblings

Hlogi

Short for *Lehlogonolo*

Hlologelo

Longing, yearning of. To miss someone or something (feel the absence or loss thereof)

Hlompho (*Tlhompho*)

Respect

Holeng

Long awaited – especially if it took the mother a very long time (years) to fall pregnant or the baby was overdue. It's been way too long / passing of time

Hopolang

Remember; remembrance

I

Ikaneng

Ikana – swear an oath; Swear by or promise solemnly

Ikemeleng

Take a stand; be independent

Ikgopoleng

Put (think of) yourselves first; remembrance

Ithaopeng

Volunteer; be determined

Ithuteng

Educate yourselves; learn or develop

Itireleng

Fend (do) for yourselves

Itumeleng

Be happy, content, glad, delighted

K

Kabelo

Share (one's share), inheritance; a gift

Kabo

A gift, share

Kabomo

Intentional

Kae

Where? How?

Kaelo / Kaelelo

Kaêla – guide; Guidance (from God); a story, tale

Kagiso

Peace, harmony, tranquillity, serenity

Kagisano

Neighbourly, living together harmoniously

Kahlolo

Judgement, condemnation

Kamanyo

Association, relation; connection, involvement

Kamo

Short form of *Kamogelo, Kamogetso*

Kamogelo (Kamohelo)

Acceptance, approval, reception; Holy Communion

Kamogetso

Welcome, embrace, approved

Karabelo

Dependability, trustworthiness, reliability

Karabo

An answer, response

Karolo

A share, part (n), section; a quota

Katafalo

Multiplication, enlargement

Katano

Battle, friction; Intensification, upsurge

Katiso

Multiplication, enlargement

Katlego

Fruitful, success, prosperity

Katliso

Successful, accomplishment, victorious

Kea

I have; short for *Keamogetswe* or Keagile

Keamogetse

I've received, accepted, embraced

Keamogetswe

(Keamogetsoe)

I've been welcomed, embraced, accepted

Kebareng

How do I respond to them - expressing confusion and amazement?

Keboabetswe

It's been bequeathed, bestowed (on me)

Kedirile

I've accomplished; done it; I'm able

Kediso

Enlightenment; clarification

Kefentse

I am victorious, triumphant; successful

Kego

I have ...

Kehumile

I am affluent, wealthy

Keikantse

I've promised, vowed, pledged

Keitso

Knowledge

Keitu

Short for *Keitumetse*

Kekeletso

Increament, amplification, addition; short form - *Keke*

Keketso (Koketso)

Increament, amplification, addition

Kelebone

It (he/she) is light; I have seen

Kelefiwe

Lefa – to pay; I've been rewarded

Kelello

Knowledgeable, intelligence

Kelikilwe

I've been tested, tried, challenged

Kenewang

Newa – to give; what am I been given?

Kenna

I am (affirmation)

Kenosi

I'm on my own; lonesome, deserted

Kentse

I'm fine, excellent (as I am), satisfied.

Keolebogile

I've thanked Him (God)

Keorapetse

I've prayed to… God

Keotshepile

I trust in Him (God)

Keratile

I've loved, wished

Kerekilwe

I've been bought,
purchased, acquired;
could signify IVF;
monetary exchange to
enable conception

Kerekere

To try it all but in vain

Kesegofetse

I've been blessed

Ketelo

Visitation

Kethabile

I am happy

Keutlwile

I've had enough; I've
learned a lesson; I've
understood

Kgabo (Khabo)

Monkey, Ape; also a
flame or a torch

Kgalalelo

Adoration, exaltation,
luminosity; holiness

Kgaogelo (Khauhelo)

Mercy; compassion,
leniency

Kgathatso

Bothersome, exasperate,
tiresome

Kgethang (Khethang)

Choose, elect

Kgolego

Delayed; jail

Kgomo

Cow

Kgomotso (K*h*omotso)

Console, comfort,
condolence

Kgopelo

A Request

Kgopotso

Remembrance,
commemoration

Kgwerano

Covenant, friendship

Kholofelo

Hope

Khotso (K*g*otso)

Peace

Khotsofalang
(K*g*otsofalang)

Be content, satisfied

Khumo

Wealth

Khutsang

Be at peace, peaceful

Kitso

Knowledge

Koketso

Addition

Kolobe

A pig

Kopang

Ask, request

Kopano

Unity

Kopelo

Song, hymn; a request
especially in prayer

Kutlwano (Kutloano)

Unity; agreement
(mutual)

Kutlwisiso

Understanding

Kutullo

To bring to light, delve
into; revelation

L

Leabua

You are talking,
discussing, conversing

Leago

Pillar, building

Lebalang

Forget; put it out of your
mind

Leballo

Forgiveness

Lebitsa

Bitso – the name; the
one to be known; one
who attracts attention,
commands respect or
makes people take
notice. A call

Lebo

Short for *Lebogang*

Lebona

A visionary

Leboga (s)

Be grateful, thankful; pet
form *Lebo*

Lebogang (p)

Be grateful, thankful

Ledile

Awaiting; the awaited one

Lefelana

Lefela – nothing; of nothing; a small nothing. *Lefa* – inheritance; a small inheritance Could also mean to pay; to square it up or make payment to each other

Lefentse

You've triumphed, succeeded, conquered; pet form *Fefe*

Lefihlile

Fihla – to arrive; he/she have arrived. Also

means to hide – you've hidden…

Lefilwe

You've been given, allocated

Lefu (Leso)

Death, misfortune; one born of/from death or after a death in the family

Legae

A home / abode; shows stability, reliability

Lehlogonolo

Blessing

Lekweng

Listen and understand; pay attention, take heed; hear, hope one's learned from one's mistakes

Lemoha

Be aware, perceptive; take heed

Lemohang (Lemogang)

Be aware, perceptive; take heed

Lenka

One who takes; a taker

Lentenne

Tenna – annoyance or anger; you've annoyed/angered me

Lepulana

The pale one; one of mixed heritage

Lerato (Lorato)

Love; affection

Lereng

Pardon; posing a question to the in-laws or the community 'What do you have to say now?'

Lesebo

Gift from the ancestors; gossip (*n*)

Lesedi

The light

Lesego

Luck

Leshoko

Compassion, pity

Lethabo

Happiness; short form *Thabo*

M

Maboko

Praises, poems

Mabona

A visionary; one who enlightens

Mabu

Sand, dust; dirt

Madimabe

Bad luck; cursed

Mafalelo

Go faletsa – to fill up; the act of filling up, increasing or toping up – refers to increasing the family in terms of children; also – to add up, exaggerate

Mahlakanye (Mat*lh*akanye)

One who's always confused or gets muddled up; very disorganised or creates disorganisation. One who tends to create misunderstanding?

Mahlatse (Mahlats*i*)

Luck; the fortunate one

Mahlogonolo (Mat*lh*ogonolo)

Blessings

Makalo (Maka*ll*o)

Surprise, perplexity, puzzlement

Makgatho

Divisions, gradings, sections

Makgolong

Lekgolo – a hundred; in the hundreds – could signify wealth or many children

Makgone

One who excels

Makgopo

The begrudging one; upset; also eggs

Makgora

Kgora – abundance; one who has plenty; suffice

Makgothoane

One who unsettles or turns things up side down; refers to disharmony

Malefane

Lefa – pay, one who pays one's dues

Manello

A dwelling

Mangwadi

The written word; writers

Manthatisi

Lovable

Maphanye

Phanya – to break or burst out; one who is easily angered or fierce

Mapheto

Go pheta – to repeat; symbolises another

sibling especially of the same sex; *pheto* – the end or to finish; signifies the endings therefore name given to last child

Masalesa

The remaining one; coming after

Masedi

Lights

Masego

Luck, fortune

Mashadikane

One who is confused and is unfocussed

Mashapa

Go shapa – to hit or beat up; one who likes fighting or to start fights

Mathe

Saliva, spittle

MatheaModimo

GOD's spittle i.e a blessed one

Mathuba

Go thuba – to destroy, break down; a destroyer

Matla

Strength, power

Matlakadibe

One who is sinful (*dibe*) or brings chaos and bad omen

Matlogile

Tloga – to leave, depart; one who leaves

Matshwenyego

Hardship, unpleasantness

Mefelo

Endings; the ending, closure

Mekgwa

Manners; protocol

Meloreng

Of/ in ashes (*melora*)

Merafo

Nations

Metse

Dwellings, houses

Mmela

Grow, expand; growth, pastures

Mmolawa

The victim (the dead) – the one who got killed (to hounour the dead without using their actual name)

Modumeleng

Permit or allow him/her; accept ...

Mogomaneng

Find or locate him/her

Mogomotsi

One who comforts

Mohau (Mogau)

Mercy, pity

Mohlatso

Purification, cleansing

Mohlatswa (Mohlatso)

A fruit tree
(*Chrysophyllum magaliesmontanum*)

Mohlokohloko

Extreme poverty

Mokgadi

Go kgala – to call to order, one who reprimands or chastises

Molata

One who's confrontational; also, one who fetches or a messenger

Molebatse (Molebatsi)

The one who makes others forget; one who comforts or is able to appease

Molebogeng

Thank HIM

Molelekwa

The one who is chased away; the one who's unwanted or demoted

Molemo

Satisfaction, acceptance

Molomowatau

A lion's mouth; refers to a tough and sharp person who commands respect especially when they speak

Moluleloa (Moduleloa)

The awaited one

Mongatse

A hat, covers and keeps warm; the protector

Mongwai

Go ngwaya – to scratch; the cratcher

Mongwatsona

The owner, proprietor

Monosi

A loner; alone – probably no family ties

Monthati

One who loves and cherishes me

Montsho

The dark one; a dark horse

Mooketsi

One who adds to or increases the family

Moraka

A house or dwelling. Also refers to types of gourd (*Legenaria vulgaris*)

Morapedi

One who prays; a believer

Moroka (Moroki)

A tailor

Morotola

One who causes turmoil

Mosa

Grace

Mosemodi (Mosemoli)

The initiator, starter

Moshwanatjo

Go shwa – to die; one who takes all the secrets

and knowledge with to the grave

Mosi (Mos*h*i)

Smoke

Mosodi

The suspicious one

Motheo

A foundation (beginning of a family)

Mothusi

An assistant, helper

Motlatsi

An addition to the family

Motlatso (Motla*tj*o)

Support; addition

Motodi (Mo*th*odi)

The founder; discoverer

Motseleng

On, of or by the road

Motsha (Motšha)

The young; a new person

Motswagae

A kinsman (*a homey –* slang)

Motswakae

A foreigner; not a local person

Mphete

Make it happen again; a wish to be blessed again with child; repetition; 'go ahead of me'

Mpho

A gift

Mpholletse

Heal me; restore me to health; heal for me

Mponeng

Let me be admired, seen

Mpho

A gift; also short for *Dimpho* (gifts)

Mphonyana

A small gift

Mporotle

Take me around with you; behold me

Mpotseng

Ask me; inform me, let me know

Mpua

A newborn baby

Namedi

One to rises high or who reaches a higher position in society; a social climber; a creeper

Neo

A gift or offering; also short for *Dineo* (gifts)

Ngata

Multiple, many; a bundle of ... wood

Ngwanamakala

Ngwana – a child; Child of <u>Makala</u> (surprise, amaze); refers to a surprise due to an unexpected pregnancy

Ngwanamoagi

Child of Moagi – a builder, a mason

Ngwanapedi

Child of Pedi (one who's from the North); also means second child

Ngwedi

Moon

Nkadimeng

Lend me

Nkagele

Help me build a family

Nkamang (Nkameng)

Embrace me; also mean concerns, involvement

Nkebe

If only …, denotes regret;

Also a signifies wishfulness

Nkgasha (Nkgaša, Nkgasa)

To spread around, duplicate

Nkgodiseng

Godisa – to bring up; bring me up, let me grow and develop

Nkgomeleng

Go goma – to go back, return; to take as far as …, take me part of the way, let me continue alone be independent

Nkhupetseng

Khupetsa – to cover up or hide; swaddle me, shield me

Nkoeneane (Nkoenyane, kwenyane)

Nkoe – a tiger; the dimunitive of Tiger (a small tiger)

Nkoketseng

Add on more; let there be more, bequeath more on me

Nkopeng

Kopa – to ask; ask or request of me

Nkwane

Mutual understanding

Nteme

Lema – to plough; plough me – the family's wish for bride to bear heirs

Nteseng

Let me be

Nteteng

Go leta – to wait; wait upon me; the long awaited heir / child

Nthatho

Love, desire

Ntsolo

Upliftment, encouragement

* A celebration to mark the removal of garments (black) worn during mourning where the deceased clothes could be shared amongst family members

Oamogetswe

He/she has been received, welcomed

Oagile

You/God have/has built (started a family); the child has made us a family

Oarabile

HE has answered, responded (to prayers)

Obohlale

God is wise

Odirile

HE has made it happen

Ofentse [Fentse, Fefe]

HE is victorious

Ogodile

He has grown, strengthened

Ogona

HE is present; HE exist

Oitseone

Only HE knows

Okgopetswe

This child has been asked for, requested, prayed for

Olebogeng

Thank the Lord

Olethabo

HE is happiness; there's happiness/joy

Oletlile

He/she is waited upon

Olona

You are; of yours (*pl*)

Omatla

God is powerful

Omperekajwang

'Why do/act as such towards me?' Signifies unfair treatment or change of mind after mutual agreement

Omphemetse

God has permitted (to have a child); you've protected me

Omphile

HE has given, blessed me

Ontiretse

HE has come through for me

Orapeleng

Pray to HIM

Oratile

HE has loved, wished

Oratiloe

HE is loved, has been loved

Oregolele

Let us flourish, mature, multiply

Oreteng

Praise HIM; rejoice in the Lord

Ororiseng

Praise HIM

Oteng

HE is present; HE is alive

Othabo

HE is happiness, joy

Otlotleng

Honour and respect HIM

Otsile

HE has come

Owame

HE is mine

P

Paballo

Protection (God's); conservation; mercy

Peulwane

A seedling

Pheeganyane (Phee*h*anyane)

Pheega – to deny; slight denial

Phehello (Pheello)

Persistence, perserverance

Pheletso

The end; completion, completeness

Phenyo

Victory

Pheto

Accomplishment; the end, conclusion

Phetogo (Phetoho)

Change; upheaval

Phetole

Upheaval, change; perponse

Phieha

Broken, dispruption

Phihlego

Secrecy; unseen

Phitise

To pass on

Pholoso

Salvation, saved

Phomolo

Rest, take a break

Phopholo

To pat down, to comfort, assure

Poelo

Gain; results

Pogiso (Pogišo)

Maltreatment; bothersome

Poloko

Safety, to keep safe; burial

Popego

Creation, formation

Potego

Trustworthy, reliable

Potlako

Haste

Puku

A book (an intellectual)

Puseletso

A repeat; repetition

R

Ramogelo

We've received, welcomed

Rasetja

Ray of light

Rategile

Beloved, loved one

Ratile

Loved, affectionate

Reabiloe (Reabilwe)

We've been blessed; given

Reagiseng

Help us build; plea for support in order to raise a big and united family

Reaotlotla

We praise, worship HIM

Reatlehile

We've prospered; we are successful

Reauboka

We praise HIM; we are full of praise

Rebiditswe

We've been summoned, called

Refentse

We are victorious; we've overcome

Regomoditswe

We've been consoled, comforted

Reholofetse (Re*kg*olofetse)

We are hopeful

Relahlile

We have lost; we've learned our lesson

Remaketse

We are surprised, puzzled

Rentse

We are fine, well, content

Resentse

We've tainted or messed up (refers to pregnancy out of wedlock)

Rorisang

Praise, honour

S

Sabuti

That of my brother's (possessive)

Saishago

Of the future

Seboleleng

The unmentionable; do not talk or discuss it

Seedi

A stream

Seemahale

A monument

Seeng

The one who went away; disapperance

Segomotso

That which comforts, consoles

Segopotso

Remembrance

Sehloho

Cruelty, unkindness (probably underlining ill treatment of the bride by the in-laws)

Sehlola

The victor; surreal

Sehlomi

The initiator, a starter

Sehope

Of nowhere; out of nowhere

Seipei

Self appointed

Sekgaloane

That which caused a divide; disharmony

Sekgokhana

One who is confused, muddled up; that which has separated or strayed

Sekgole

Afar; that which comes
from afar

Selalelo

Communion, supper; the
act of hunting or keeping
watch

Selebogo

A 'thank you' gift; sign of
appreciation

Senyaka

A restless person; one
who searches

Seoketso

An addition; that which
adds on ...

Sepadi

A non-achiever;
unsuccessful person

Sepaki

An affidavit; witness
statement

Sepheto

A sequel; conclusion

Seputla

Hastiness, impulsiveness

Serati

The admirer; the dearest
one

Seroto

A basket; a price

Seruwe

The kept one; a farm
animal

Setlamorago

The one who comes last
(last born); aftermath

Setswakae

'From where does she/he come?' An unexpected pregnancy especially when the couple thought they'd completed their family – a blessing nonetheless

Shitwane

That which hinders; impediment

Shupang

Shupa – points out, signifies; of significance

T

Tao

Instruction, command

Takatso

A yearning, deepest longing or wish (for a child)

Tebogo

Thanks, gratefulness

Tefelo (Tefe*ll*o)

To pay; a reward

Thaba

Be happy

Thabang

Rejoice, be happy

Thabo

Joy, elation

Thakgatso

Happiness, enjoyment, pleasure

Thapelo

Prayer, worship

Thato

Will, desire, liking

Thatoyaone

God's will

Theriso

Consultation; act of mediation

Tholang

Quieten, stay calm; find

Tholong

A place of calmness, quiet

Thomang

Go thoma – to start; (let them ...) commence, begin or start on

Thoriso

Praise, Honour

Thoto

Baggage; belongings

Thuso (Thušo)

Support, help, assistance

Thuto

Education; a learning curve

Tirelo

Deed; service

Tlabo

Confusion, perplexity

Tlalakgolo

Famine, hunger

Tlalalego

Accomplished, fullfilment

Tlhalefang	**Tlotlang**
Be wise; be aware	Show respect
Tlhapadiatla	**Tlotlêgo**
Tlhapa – to wash, *diatla* – hands; Wash one's hands off something /someone; be clean, within the law	Respect, honour, homage
	Tlotliso
	Honour
Tlhokomelo	**Tlotlo**
Care; act of caring	Praise, glorify
Tlholo	**Tokollo (Tokologo)**
Victory, success	Freedom
Tlhompho	**Tsebo**
Respect	Knowledge, insight
Tlhoriso	**Tsele (Tseele)**
Abuse; spitefulness	A friend; companion
Tlogang	**Tsele (Tseele)**
Depart; leave	To take from or after

Tsheledi

Crossing over; after sunrise; going to bed early hours of the morning

Tseleng

On the road

Tshediso (Tsh*i*diso / Tsediso)

Condolences, sympathy; Comfort, console

Tshele

Sunrise; awakening (Tshel**é**)

Argumentative, confrontational (Tsh**êlê**)

Tshenolo

Revelation; last Book of the New Testament

Tsheo (Tshe*g*o)

Short for *Tshegofatso* - blessing

Tshepo (T*s*epo)

Hope, trust

Tshepang (T*s*epang)

Hope that ... or trust in

Tshiamo (Tsheamo)

Goodness, satisfaction, pleasant

Tshireletšo

Protection

Tshokologo

Repentant, contritite

Tsholang

Give birth; procreate, multiply; carry

Tsholanang

Carry each other, help each other

Tsholofelo

Hope

Tshupo

A sign; point out

Tshwanelo

Rightful, befitting; appropriate

Tshwarelo

Forgiveness

Tshwaro

A gathering; incarceration, apprehend

Tshwenyego

Apprehensive; worried

Tsietso

Dilemma; perplexity

Tšoeu (T*sweu*/ Ts*hw*eu)

White; the white one (light skinned)

Tsotang

Amazement

Tsoselletso

To awaken; to give life to, to repeat

Tswaledi

The last one, closure

Tumelo

Faith, consent, belief

Tumi

Short for *Tumelo*, *Tumiso, Tumisang*

Tumishi

Praise

Tumiso (Tumisho)

Praise

Tumisang

Praise HIM

W

Waamogeloa

He/she has been
received, welcomed

Wabona

Theirs; belongs to them

Waipshina

Go ipshina – to enjoy;

Self enjoyment, self
appreciation

Wanthata

God loves me; I am
loved, adored

Warona

Ours (the child)

Wasello

Of tears (*sello*), born
during or after a sad
period for the family
maybe death

Watsholo

Of birth

Watumelo

Of belief

Wetsho (Weetsho)

Ours; kinsman

Banana

Banyana

Kgadi

Lekgarebe

Makgarebe

Mofumagadi

Mohumagadi

Morwetsana

Mosadi

Mosetsana

Mma/Mme

Ngwanyana

Ousi

Sesi

GIRLS NAMES

A

Abile

Shared, bequethed

Agesho (Agešo)

Ours

Akamiya

Aka (v) to carry;
someone who carries or
helps one through tough
times

Akanang

Help mould or help each
other (family)

Atile

Procreated, multiplied

B

Babotseng

In/of beauty; surrounded
by beauty

Baetesi

From B*aeti* - visitors; one
who brings or makes
people visit

Basajana (*dim*)

Basadi – women; young,
little women (*basatsana*)

Basetsana

Girls; another girl born

Bathabile

They're happy, joyous

Bohlokwa (Bohlokoa)

Of importance, precious

Boikanyo

Rely upon, trusted

Boikarabelo

Responsibility; take charge

Boikgantso

Pride/proud, vanity

Boikhutso

Khutsa – to rest; restfulness; peacefulness

Boipelo

Pride, honour, self respect, dignity

Boithekgo

Ithekga – lean (v); pillar,

backing, encouragement

Boitlhakile

Hlakile – clear; clarity, clearness

Boitshepo

Tshepo – hope; hopefulness

Boitshoko (Boichoko)

Perseverance

Boitshupo

Ability to prove, show

Boitumelo

Happiness, joy

Boledi

A discussion, talk

Bolelle

Gentle, soft (gentleness)

Bonolo

Ease, calm, light, mild

Bontle

Beauty; good looking

Bose

Delicious

Botle

Beauty

Botse

Beauty; fine

Botsana

Beautiful

Buang

Talk, discuss;
communicate

D

Diapeng

Talk or voice it out,
discuss issues at hand

Didi

Short for *Didintle* or
Dintle though often used
as it is

Didintle

T'is beautiful, pretty,
lovely, magnificent

Dieketseng

Multiply, extend

Dikeledi (*Likeleli*)

Tears due to sadness or
unhappiness; sorrowful

Diketso (*Liketso*)

Deeds, actions – God's wish; Acts – 5th book of the New Testament (Bible)

Dikgaogelo

Lots of mercy, compassion, leniency

Dikhutso

Lots of - peace, silence, rest (a vacation)

Dikoti

Dimples; also holes, gaps, cavities

Dileseng

Let it be, leave it

Dillo

Lamentations – Old book of theTestament; tears

Dimakatso (*Limakatso*)

A marvel; surprises

Dimpho (*Limpho*)

Gifts, offerings

Dineo (*Lineo*)

Gifts, offerings

Dintle (*Lintle*)

T'is (they're) beautiful

Dioketso (Ketso)

Expansion, increment, amplification

Dipalesa (*Lipalesa*)

Flowers

Dipolelo

Talk, gossip, hearsay

Dipuo

Talk, hearsay; language

Disebo (*Lisebo*)

Gossips, rumours, tales;
whispers

Disekeletso

To savour, treasure

Diseko

Trials

Ditebogo

Gratitute, gratefulness,
appreciation

Dithato

Wishes, affections

Ditshebo

Gossips, rumours, tales;
whispers

**Ditshego (Ditshe*ho* /
Lit*šeho*)**

Laughter, happiness

**Ditshehoana
(*Litšehoana*)**

Little/tiny laughter; giggle

**Ditshwanelo
(Ditswanelo)**

That which is suitable,
appropriate

E

Eentle

It's beautiful

Elotilwe (Elotiloe)

It has been glorified;
treasured

Eoketse

Multiply, add on;
enhance

Eneiloe (Eneilwe)

It's been given,
bequeathed upon

Esêdi

T'is light, radiant

F

Felleng

Ending

Folang

Line up (wish for many
children); also mean get
well

Fumane

Founded upon,
discovered

G

Gabaikangwe

They are not trustworthy,
unreliable

Gabaiphiwe

They do not bestow upon
themselves; God is the
only who gives us.

Gabanthathe

I am unloved

Gaborone

Our home or place; also
the capital of Botswana

Gadifele

It's incessant (adj),
continuous, non stop

Gaikanelwe

Ikana – to trust, vow;

s(he) is not trustworthy;
cannot be reliable on

Gaisang

Excel, shine; outshine,
surpass

Galaletsang

Halalela (v) – holy; make
holy

Gobuamang

Bua (v) – to talk; 'who is
talking?' after a lot of
gossiping and something
good happens to silence
them (relatives)

Goitsemang
(Goitsimang)

Itse – to know; 'who
knows?' An affirmation to
say only God knows

I

Ibitsong

It's in the name (*bitso*)

Idintle

It is beautiful, beauty

Ikemeleng

Take a stand; be
independent

Ikgantse (s)

Have pride; be proud

Ikgantseng (pl)

Have pride; be proud

Ikhutseng

Have a break, rest

Ipeleng

Be proud, pleased or
joyous

Ipuseng

Guide, rule or govern yourselves

Itireleng

Tiro – work; fend (do) for yourselves

Itumeleng

Be happy, content, glad, delighted

Kananelo

Recount, relate (a story/tale); explanation

Kangwe

Short for *Gabaikangwe* – they are untrustworthy

Keabetswe (Keabetsoe)

I've been given (my share); it has been bestowed, bequeathed upon me

Keagile

Aga (v) – to build; I have firmly build, nurtured, reared, created (the family). Name often given to the last sibling

Keamogetse

I have welcomed, embraced, accepted

Kebarileng

What have I said /did I say to them?

Keboabetswe

It's been bequeathed, bestowed (on me)

Kebusitswe

I've been returned
(probably from the in-
laws)

Kedibone

I've seen, witnessed,
perceived; I've suffered -
at the hands of (the in-
laws)

Kediemetse

I've persevered or
survived tough/trying
times

Kefedi

Completed, done; for the
last born child

Kefilwe (Kefiloe)

I've been given; it's been
bestowed, bequeathed
upon me

Kefuoe

I've been given; it's been
bestowed, bequeathed
upon me

Keitumetse

I am happy, joyous

Kelebogile

I am grateful, thankful

Kelopilwe

I've been trusted
(entrusted with)

Kemane

'It's my aunt' honouring a
maternal aunt without
using their actual name
often as they've passed
on

Kemontle

I'm beautiful

Kenalemang

'Who do I have?' Name given usually after death in a family; person left all alone

Keneilwe (Keneil*oe* / Kene*h*iloe)

I've been given, blessed

Keneuwe (Keneo*ue*)

I've been given

Keromamang

'Who do I send?' A messenger; child seen as a messenger from God

Kesedi

Enlightenment

Kesegofetse

I've been blessed

Kethabile

I am happy

Ketso

An act or deed; actions

Kgadi

Girl, female

Kgahliso (K*h*ahliso)

Appeal; attraction, beauty

Kgaka

A guinea fowl (praise name)

Kgapatsana

Kgapa – to walk half way; *tsana* denotes female. A female escort, shepherdess

Kgarebe

Young lady; mature maiden who has not undergone initiation

Kgomoadira

Kgomo - bride price (*lobola*) or dowry; *adira* – done/agreed, surety that the dowry will come or be brought

Kgomogoroga

Kgomo - bride price (*lobola*) or dowry; g*oroga* – arrival; cattle arrive - it's the family hope that their child will get married one day and bring home a sizeable dowry

Kgorosi

Arrival (baby), presence; ushering in (signifies arrival of cows or lobola)

Kgosatsana

A queen [feminine of *Kgosi* (king)]

Kgosiyadikobo

King (though female, used if there's no male lineage or succession to the throne) of the ugly, unsightly; no good

Kgothatso (K*h*othatso)

Console, comfort, reassurance; encouragement

Kgotsofatso

Appease, satisfaction

Khudu

A tortoise (praise name)

Koko

Grandmother; named in honour of the grandmother

Kutloisiso (Kutlwisiso)

Understanding; considerate; self awareness

L

Larona

Ours (He/she is ours)

Lebone

Light

Lelentle

She's beautiful; the beautiful one

Leoneetsoe

You've been blessed

Letsatsi

The sun; a day

Liepollo (Diepollo)

Revelations, exposure

Likhapha (Dikgapha)

Tears (mournful)

Liseli (Disedi)

Lights

Liwetse

T'is fallen, succumbed

Lolo

From the English name Lorraine but now widely used as a Sotho name

M

Maborwa

Borwa – the South; a
lady from the South

Mabotse

Botse – beauty; the
beautiful one, a beauty
queen

Mabusha

The conqueror, ruler

Madichaba

Mother of the nation

Madiganeng

A very argumentative
one

Madika (Ma/ika)

A poet; a narrator

Madikoko

Dikoko – roosters or
chickens; one who
owns/works with poultry
(a trade name)

Madiponto

Diponto – slang for
money; one with lots of
money or born to
money/wealth

Madisha

A sherperdess, a herd-
girl

Maditibele

Ditebele – boxing or fists;
a fighter or lady who can
use her fists;

Go tibela – to chase
away; one who chases

others away or one who's forever in chase

Maditsebe

Ditsebe – ears; one with massive ears (physical attributes); a great listener or one who hears and knows all secrets

Maeteletsa

Eletsa – to advice; self-adviser; guru or counsellor

Magadi (Ma*h*adi)

Lobola, dowry, bride price

Magalela

The one who shines – a star; the Holy one

Magauta

Gauta – gold; a lady with lots of gold or Money; has expensive taste

Mahlako (Mahlak*u*)

Branches (leaves)

Mahlasedi

Rays of light

Mahlodi

Go hlola – to create; the creator (mother earth)

Mahlogo

Hlogo – a head i.e the family head;

Could also be a physical attribute - one with a massive head; intelligent one

Maikeletsi

Eletsa – to advice; self advises; insightful

Makaepea

Self elected

Makanama

Go kanama – to laze around; one who just lies around doing nothing; a lazy person

Makau

Name given to honour Mrs. (*Ma*) <u>Kau</u> (surname) who could have been a great help or influence to the family

Makaukau

Kaukau is a plant *Coccinia rehmanii* – name could have been shortened to *Kau* which will then refer to a lady (*Ma*) who deals with *kaukau* (trade name); pet form *Makau*

Makgabo

Kgabo – a monkey (praise name), mother of <u>Kgabo</u>; could also mean a spark or flame – one who sparkles or lights up the room

Makgamo

Go kgama – to milk; a trade name – one who milks the cows thus, a milk lady; could be one in charge of getting water from the river – capable of feeding the family as water is an important resource

Makgang

The stubborn one

Makgapile

One who accompanies –
could be the remaining
twin; a female guide

Makgare

Kgare – a wreath or
burning flames, one who
is lively and interesting.
Could signify a child born
after a death in a family
or mother died during
child birth

Makgatlha

Kgatlha – to like; the
likeable, attractive or
desirable one

Maki

Short for *Dimakatso* - a

Marvel; surprises

Makoma

Koma – initiation
ceremony where boys
and pubertal girls attend
to be initiated into
adulthood; principal wife
of tribal chief in charge of
the girls' (*byale*) initiation

Makorong

Koro – wheat; a trade
name for one who works
with wheat

Makoti

A bride

Makoto (Mak*utu***)**

Koto (kutu) – a trunk of a
tree, signifies strength;
one who sustains and
nurtures; a provider

Malebelo

Lebelo – speed; one who will be a fast runner – the one with speed

Malebo

Thanks, appreciation

Malebogo

Gratefulness, thanks

Malebone

Lebone – light; the radiant one

Malefo (Malef*u* / Male*h*u)

Lefu (lehu) – death; one born of death or after a death in the family; mother of death

Malehlogonolo

The blessed one

Malehumo

Lehumo – wealth; one of the many daughters which means more cattle and hence wealth; one born into wealth

Maleshoane

Ladybird

Maletjatji (Maletsatsi)

Letjatji – the sun; born at daylight often after an extended labour

Maletsholo

Go tshola – to carry or give birth; one who will carry the weight of the family

Malohle

Lohle – all; mother of all or everyone

Mamafolo

Mafolo – energy; the energetic one

Mamare (Mama*the*)

Mare/mathe – spittle (saliva); one who produces a lot of spittle; a baby who dribbles (slobbers) a lot

Mamello

To listen – a good listener; patience

Mamere

Mere – tears; a child who cries incessantly

Mammopu

Mmopu – maize; a trade name probably works in a maize-field or sells maize

Mamohau

The merciful and kind-hearted one

Mamohlabane

A female warrior

Mamolete

Molete – a hole; probably a trade name for one who digs or works in a mine

Mamollo

Mollo – fire; one who will be fiery, exciting

Mamose

The one from overseas (foreigner)

Mamoratwa

The beloved, the loved one

Mamoraka

Moraka – house, dwelling; the lady of the house

Mampe (Mamp*i*)

Mpe – ugly, awful, bad; the unfortunate one or one shrouded by misfortune; mother of calamity

Mampotshe

Go botsa – to question; one who questions or has an enquisitive mind

Manase

A lady nurse (nase); child named after the nurse who may have taken good care of the mother while in hospital

Mangwato

Bechuana cattle which make heavy and powerful trek oxen

Mankepeng

Go epa – to dig; one who digs; an investigator or one who attempts to find solutions

Mankgana

Gana – to refuse or deny; a child who has been rejected by the family while mother was pregnant; one who turns their back away from or refuses (me)

Mankopane

Kopane – to meet; one who brings people (family) together;

harmonious person;

kopa – to ask, one who's constantly asking for or borrowing from others

Manoke

A restless one, never sits still nor stays in one area

Mantebeng

Go leba – to stare; one who likes attention or will draw attention to herself, exhibitionist; attractive

Manthotho

Thotho – belongings; one who carries or has lots of stuff; cluttersome

Mantoa (Mantwa)

One who likes to fight or confrontational

Mantseleng

Tsela – a road, a traveller; one who's always on the road

Mantsho (Mantso)

The dark one; one with dark skin

Mapaseka

Paseka – Easter; one born at Easter

Mapelo

Pelo – heart; one who's goodhearted

Maphefo

Phefo – wind; one who brings blustery weather or is born on a windy day

Maphoko

Phoko – dew; one born on a dew-coated day (very cold day)

Maphoshane

Go phosha – to throw; a thrower or one who passes ... (information) around

Mantsha

Ntsha – to reveal; one with foresight

Maphefo

Phefo – the wind; one who brings winds

Mapula (Mapule)

Pula – rain; one who brings the rain (rainy weather) welcomed as it is good for fields/ crops

Marelete

Go leta – to wait; the awaited one

Marokana

Roka – to sew; a tailor

Marona

Our mother (*Ma*); mother of the community

Masana

'*Go sana sana*' to idle around especially outside the homestead

Maseabe

Aba – to divide; one who will help divide; a beneficiary

Maseboshego

Boshego – night time; a night owl

Maselebalo

Selebalo – forgiveness; one with a forgiving heart

Masello

Sello – tears; one who cries or wails incessantly

Masemenya

Go menya – to implore, beseech; one who's constantly imploring

Mashiko

Shiko is nothing, mother of nothing

Mashikoane

A small mother of nothing (*shiko*) the dimunitive of *Mashiko*, a name given to a second or smallest twin the first one being *Mashiko*

Masidiye

Go diya – to do; the non-doer or one who doesn't perform

Masehlomeng

Go hloma – to anchor, also to start; an achor; a starter

Masetene

Setene – taken from the Afrikaans <u>Steyn</u>; named to honour Mrs Steyn who may have made a huge impact in parent's life; *Seteno* – also means annoyance; one who's easily annoyed

Masetshaba

Mother of a nation (*setshaba*)

Mashadi

Mother of a girl / female (*shadi*) child

Mathabo

One who's happy (*thabo*), delighted

Mathapelo

Woman of prayer (a church goer)

Matho*tho* (Mathoto)

One with lots of baggage or luggage

Matlakala

Waste, rubbish - popular name given to a child born after death of another sibling or following a miscarriage; also means pages of a

book which signifies an academic or intellectual

Matsaka

Tsaka – mine; mother of my clan/children (very affectionate way of saying my wife)

Matsatsi

Tsatsi – the sun or day time; born when the sun was shining

Matsela / Matseleng

A traveller; a voyager

Matshidiso

Condolences; child born after death in the family whose birth will console the family; short form *Tshidi*

Matshilo

Tshilo - an upper grinding stone; a grinder (trade name)

Matutu

Juice, nectar, sweetness - nectar of the gods; could also refer to Mrs. <u>Tutu</u>

Maune

Fruits; could also be *mother of Une* which is taken from the Irish name <u>Una</u> (lamb)

Mayagaba (Moya*h*abo**)**

One who decides to return home; signifies the bride's return when the marriage is over or has been ill-treated

Mmabagwe

Their mother 'mother of his own'

Mmabatho

Mother of the people (nation)

Mmabontle

The beautiful one or a beauty queen

Mmadika

A poet or narrator

Mmaditaba

One who brings news; an informer

Mmaditshelete

One with money or wealthy

Mmahlale

Hlale – thread; a seamstress

Mmamma (*M*amma)

Mother of my mother; honouring the parent's grandmother without using her name due to a recent death

Mmagobatho

B*atho* – people; mother of the people, a leader

Mmakoma

Mother of *Koma* (initiation)

Mmakosi (Mmak*g*osi)

Mother of the king (*Kgosi*) – the queen

Mmamose

One from overseas (*mose*); a foreigner

Mmampe

The unfortunate one or one shrouded by misfortune; queen of calamity; mother of war

Mmarona

Rona – us; our mother; referring to a prominent female figure

Mmasaka

Saka – mine; mother of my … children, lot, clan

Mmangwako

Ngwako – a house; the owner or wife of the owner of that household; lady of the house

Mmantsha

One who takes out; an ushrette

Mmathobele

Wife of Motsha (Thobele's brother) the son of Chief Tabane of the Maroteng clan; mother of *Thobele*

Mmatlala

Tlala – hunger, famine; one who's always hungry or brings hunger; child born during a famine

Mmoke (Mook*i*)

A healer, a nurse

Mmule

Bula – to open or start; the one who does the opening; name given to the first born child

Modiegi

The belated one; a baby delayed in coming or being born

Modjadji

A famous rain queen from Lebowa in the Northern Province of South Africa

Mogaleadi

Mogale – a brave person; a heroine

Mofubetsoana

Sefuba – chest; one who vows by hitting their chest in earnest; the beloved (bossom)

Mogolodi

A blue crane (praise name)

Mohorosi (Mogôrôsi)

Pied Barbet (*Lybius leucomelas*); also one who arrives or brings home …

Moipone

An arrogant, aloof person; self admirer, a snob

Moirapula

The rain maker (born after drought)

Mokekolo

The old woman i.e honouring the grandmother

Mokete

Celebration, a feast

Mokgadi

Kgadi – female, of womanhood

Molatlhoe

Latlha – to throw away, the unwanted one; also the lost one – child named after a relative who vanished and never heard of

Molebaleng

The one to be forgotten; forget him/her; do not think of him/her

Montlenyana

Bontle – beauty; the beautiful one

Montshiwa

The one who is taken out; one seen as a bride

Mookodi

A rainbow

Morakane

A small house, dwelling

Morariseleng

Discuss or confer in her favour

Morateng

Let her be loved, admired

Moratwa

The beloved

Moroesi (Morwesi)

One who carries or bears the burden (of the family)

Morongwa (Morongoa)

A messenger; an angel

Morongwanyana

A small angel; a young messenger

Mosadi

A woman, lady

Mosemotsane

The beautiful one

Mosetsane

A girl

Mosetsanagape

Another girl

Mošidi (Moshidi)

A cinder; grinder; also a tree with medicinal value (*Ximenia caffra*)

Mosima

A ditch; one who tends the fields

Mosimodi

A starter; initiator, inventor

Mosopyadi

A female guide or advisor

Mothabeleng

Be happy for or rejoice with her

Mothepane

A young woman who'd undergone initiation

Motholeli (Mothole*d*i)

Thola – to be quiet; the quiet or gentle one, uncomplicated person;

also *Thola* – to find; the founder, inventor

Motlagomang

One who comes or arrives to no-one in particular; leisurely arrive

Motlalepula

One who brings rain

Motlalethabo

One brings happiness, joy

Motlatso

Tlatsa – to fill up; Fulfilment, an accomplishment

Motle

Beautiful

Motleleng

Tlela – bring for; a wish for a girl to born into the family; a sign of offertory

Motsebone

Their home; homely

Motselisi (Mot*shidi*si)

One who comforts or sympathises (condolences); mourners

Mots*h*abi (Motsabi)

The one who runs away, flees; never sticks around long enough

Motshepiseng

Make her a promise

Motshodisi

A care taker; a bearer

Motsoedi (Mots*w*edi)

A spring; a fountain

Motumiseng

Praise HIM

Moyagabo (Mea*h*abo)

One who returns home

Mpheng

Bless or bequeathe upon me

Mphiwa

The receiver

Mpitseng

Call me (call for me)

Mponele

Put forward to be admired; observe on my behalf

Mponeng

Admire me; behold me

Mpsana

A young ostrich

N

Nakedi

Pole cat (praise name)

Naledi

Star, eternal

Namane

A calf

Nane

Fairy tale, story

Naume (Naome)

Taken from the English
Naomi

Ngakoana

A small house,
household

Ngokoane (Ngokwane)

Small dwelling, a hut

**Ngwakwana
(Ngwakoana)**

Small dwelling, a hut

Ngwanana

Girl, girl child

Ngwetsane

Ngwedi – the moon; the
dimunitive of ngwedi, a
small moon

Nkele

Short form of *Dikeledi* (tears)

Nkeng

Take me; a wish to be part of a family

Nkgabe

Beautify, revamp

Nkgadi

Young lady, girl

Nkgetheleng

Choose for me

Nkitsing

Itsi – know; let me be known; plead to be acknowledged by the family (more so on the paternal side)

Nkobala

To calm down; to hush

Nkobe

Chase away; disperse of

Nkoko

The old lady (*koko*) in the possessive; grandmother

Nkone

Of the North; lady from the North

Nkotsane

A small nose; bewildered by the size of the nose

Nnese

Taken from the English word nurse (trade); child named after a nurse who's name is unknown as a sign of appreciation

Ntebaleng

Forget me; could also mean forgiveness

Ntebo

Pet form of *Ntebogeng*, give thanks

Ntebogeng

Thank me; give thanks

Nteleki

Leleka – to chase away; one who chases others away and with whom it is difficult to get along

Ntepeng

Go tepa – to spoil or be spoiled; one who is spoiled / a brat - be lenient; *nthepeng* – of girls or femininity

Nthabeleng

Be happy for me; rejoice with me

Nthabiseng

Make me happy; an informal prayer or secret wish to get the gender for which the family is hoping

Nthane

To impart, pass on

Nthateng

Love and adore me

Nthele

Spoken; addressed

Nthepa

A young pubertal girl

Nthepane (Nth*i*pane)

The back of an apron mothers or guardians often give to their daughters to wear to their initiation ceremony; refers also to one who is girl like, angelic

Nthepeng

Of the young ladies; the clothing of a young lady worn to the initiation ceremony

Ntholeng

Find me; also means to carry or bear

Nthupang (Ntho*p*eng)

Go thopa – to conquer; conquered (conquer me)

Ntladi

Tladi – thunder; of thunder or one born on a thunderous day

Ntsebeng

Let me be known; pronouncement

Ntshepiseng

Promise me; pledge your support

Nyakallo

Joy

Ntswaki

Name given to a girl child who is to grow up amongst boys (princess)

Ntswelengwe

One voice (*lentswe*); signifies unity

Oarona (Warona)

She's ours

Obontle

She's beauty (beautiful)

Ompabaletse

HE has proctected, sheltered or shielded me

Oneile

HE has given; has bequeathed upon

Onkamotse

HE has taken away from me; I've been disarmed

Onkarabetse

He has answered for me (through prayer)

Onkatlile

Atla – to kiss or embrace; HE has embraced me; HE has blessed me

Onkamile

Kama – to carry; HE has carried me; HE has involved me

Onthatile

HE has loved or shown love to me

Orebabaletse

Paballo – protection; HE has protected us (is proctecting us)

Osedi

HE (God) is light (*Lesedi*)

Osiame

GOD is good

Ousi (Ausi)

Big sister; as a sign of
respect for an older
female sibling or in
honour of an older
female relative

P

Palesa

Flower

Paseka

Easter

Pelonomi

Good hearted; of one's
heart

Phahamo

Elevation (of status),
eminence

Phaladi

A female antelope

Phatsimo

One who glows or
sparkles; one who shines
– could mean success

Pheladi

Phela – to live; the one
full of life (praise name)

Phemelo

Permission; protection

Phethegile

Accomplished; has been
done or God's will has
been done

Phokane

Phoka – dew; small amount of dew

Phomello

Success, triumphant

Ponatshego

Visible, in the open

Pudigadi

Female goat (doe)

Pueng

In discussion or where there are discussions; whispers

Pulane

Rainy

Puleng

In the rain

Pusang (*Busang*)

Rule, govern

Puseletso

Repetition

Putsiso

A question

R

Raesetsa

Of light; derived from *Lesetsa* (ray of light) but made feminine

Raesibe (Ra*i*sibe)

Siba is a pet form for Lesiba (feather); by putting **Ra** and an **e**, the name becomes feminine, one as light as a feather

Ramadimetsa

(Ramadimetʝa)

Madi (blood), *metsa* (to swallow); honouring a male relative called Madimetsa (surname)

Ramadiwe

Honouring male relative called Madiwe (surname)

Ramahatsane

Honouring male relative called Mahatsane (surname); *hatsa* (to spread) – one who spreads

Ramaila

Honouring male relative called Maila (to react to certain foods) i.e with allergies

Ramaisela

Honouring male relative called Maisela; *isa* – to take; one who takes or brings

Ramakoka

Honouring male relative called Makoka (round balls of cooked stiff maize porridge or pap)

Ramalesela

Honouring male relative called Malesela; *Go lesa* – to let be or leave behind; one who leaves someone behind or a starter but never completes

Ramaredi

Go reela – to name after; the namesake. Also in

honour of a male relative called Maredi *(Mare – spittle; slippery one)*

Ramasela

Honouring male relative called Masela *(sela - to pick up; one who picks up)*

Ramasere

Honouring male relative called Masere (surname)

Ramashadi

Honouring a male relative called Mashadi *(shadi – female)*

Ramasilele

Honouring male relative called Masilele *(sila – to grind); one who grinds or works with grinders)*

Ramatitsane

Titsana – to meet or come across;

Honouring male relative called Matitsane (one who unites)

Ramatsabane

Honouring male relative called Matsabane

Ramatsimela

Honouring male relative called Matsimela

Ramatsobane

Honouring male relative called Matsobane *(Matsoba – flowers)*

Ramokone (Kone)

Bokone – the north, from the North; in honour of a

male relative called Mokone (of the north)

Ramolokwane

Honouring male relative called Molokwane (a small nation)

Ramolwetsi

Honouring male relative called Molwetsi (a sick person, patient)

Ramosele

Honouring male relative called Mosele (a tail) and *sele* - dawn

Ramoshoeu

Honouring male relative called Moshoeu (one with light skin tone or a white person; also name of a Basotho chief)

Rankaelang

Honouring male relative called Nkaelang (guidance)

Rapaledi

Honouring male relative called Paledi (unsuccessful or of difficulty)

Rapulana

Honouring male relative called Pule (mild rain)

Ratelô

Of love

Reabetswe

We've been bequeathed; we've inherited

Realeboga

We are grateful

Rebone

We've seen, observed

Rebotile

Bota – glorify; we've worshipped, glorified

Refilwe

Go fa (v) – to give; we've been given

Reitumetse

We are joyful, happy

Relebogile

We are grateful

Relopile

Go lopa - to honour and take care of; we've honoured, taken good care of

Reneilwe

Go ne(y)a (v) – to give, offer, bless; we've been blessed, given

Reshoketswe (Reshoketse)

Leshoko – mercy; we've been shown mercy, empathy

Retsilisitsoe (Retshidisitswe)

We have been consoled (often after death in the family)

S

Sanku

Nku - a sheep; one who exhibits sheep-like attributes; of sheep

Sarona

Ours; it's ours (the child)

Sebetlane

Betla – to carve; beauty that seems to have been carved to perfection

Sebina

A dancer, a performer

Sebolelo

Gossip, whispers; that which is discussed

Sebotsane

A beautiful one

Sebotse

Beauty; T'is beautiful

Seelang

Flowing (fluid) as a river flows

Seeletso

Advice, guidance

Seetsa

Ray of light

Sefora

Derived from the English name Sephora; could also mean French

Segametsi

One who draws water; one who will give life, sustain necessities

Seipati

Go pata (v) – to hide; the hidden one; one who hides, stays out of sight

Seipone

One who is vain, aloof, conceited

Selaelo

A command, rule; also that which signifies departure or is final

Selebaleng

'Do not forget'; remembrance

Selebogeng

Give thanks

Sellwane

One who wails; cries a lot (a cry baby)

Selogadi

That of womanhood

Semakaleng

'Don't be amazed'; the expected one

Sesana /Sesiyane

A young girl; a younger sister

Sesupo

A sign, symbol

Setumiso

Tumo – praise; the act of praising

Shoki

Short form for *Reshoketswe* – we've been shown empathy, mercy

T

Takatso

Desire, wish

Teballo (Tebalelo)

Forgiveness

Tebatso

Forgetful, distraction

Tebego

Announcement, pronouncement

Tebello

Expectation; a vigil

Tebano

Suitable; justly, justifiable

Thabile

Happy, joyful

Thari

To carry a baby on one's back with a cloth – to comfort; a carrier (papoose)

Tidimatso

To quieten, comfort; the act of keeping quiet or of creating peace, serenity

Tidimallo

Silence, quietness, serenity

Tiisetso (Tisetso)

Affirmation, strengthen, assurance

Tiragelo

Materialise, transpire

Tlakale

Short form of *Matlakala*
–waste; name often
given to siblings who are
born after the death of
the one before

Tsaboene

Theirs; that which
belongs to her family

Tsagae

Hers

Tselane

Tsela – a path, road; a
small road, an alley way

Tseletse

Taken after

**Tshegofatso
(Segofatso)**

Blessing

Tshepiso (Tsepiso)

Promise

Tshimollo

The beginning

Tshireletšo

Protection, shield

Bašemane

Basimane

Lekau

Lesogana

Lethaka

Makau

Mathakga

Monna

Mošemane

Moshanyana

Mosimanyana

Masogana

Njita

Ntate

BOYS NAMES

A

Amose

Derived from the English name Amos

Akanyang

Be thoughtful, considerate

Asemonye

Monye – alone; not alone or singleton (wish for many children)

Asêre

Taken from the English name Usher

B

Bafana

Boys, lads, young men

Bakang

Praise, the Lord

Bakwena (Bakoena)

One of the Tswana clans and *Kwena* (crocodile) is their totem

Basimane

Boys, young men

Bataung

One of the major baSotho clan whose totem is *Tau* (a lion)

Bohlokwa (Bohlokoa)

Precious

Baholo

The elders

Butinyane

Buti – brother; *nyane* –
little; little brother

Dikgapa

Tears (mournful)

Dikotsi (*Likotsi*)

Dangers; accidents

Ditaba

News, Matter, case,
dispute

D

Dieto

Visitation (visits); trips –
a traveller

Dikgang

Matter, case, news,
dispute

H

Hlôlô

Red hare

Hlolo

Defeat

Hlweko

Pure, purity

110

J

Jalong

Then ...; also, of the fields or pastures

Jeromo

Taken from the name Jerome

Joang (Jwang)

How (expressing disbelief); in what sense?

Josefa

Taken from the English name Joseph

Jonase

Taken from the English name Jonah

K

Kabu

Son of a Pedi chief Thobele and also father to Thobele II and Thobejane

Kau

Short for *Lekau* - a gentleman or a boy; a popular name for the dominant twin boy

Kemiso

Determination; upliftment

Keletso (Kelêtsô)

Advice

Kerefese

Taken from the English name Griffiths

Kgalang

Call to order, give warning

Kgalema

Reprimand, give warning

Kgalemo

Warning, caution, admonish

Kgang

A feud

Kgantso (Kgant*sho*)

Pride

Kgasago

Kgasa – to spread; that which has been spread around (sowed)

Kgethang

Choose

Kgetho (K*h*etho)

Choice; election

Kgodiso (Kg*u*diso / Kg*o*dis*h*o)

Growth; development

Kgokedi (Kgogedi)

A green water snake

Kgone

Done, complete

Kgopiso

Hurt, offend, upset; wound

Kgosi

King, chief

Kgosietsile (Kgositsile)

The King (son) has arrived

Kgwale

A Francolin (Natal) –
Francolinus natelensis

Kgwara

A burden; baggage

Khotso (Kgotso)

Peace

Khulong

Pastures (signifies a
good life ahead)

Kotsi

Danger, threat, menace

Kutlo

Understanding;
agreement

Kutlwisiso (Kutloisiso)

Understanding

Kwena

Crocodile

Kwenani (Kwenane)

A small crocodile

L

Leeto

A journey

Leetwane (Leetoane)

A short journey

Lefa

Inheritance (often goes
to the son/s)

Lefase

The world; the earth

Legodi (Legôdi)

Glossy Starling
(*Lamprotornis nitens*)

Lehana

Hana – to refuse; one
who refuses or is
oppositional

**Lehlabankoe
(Lehlabankwe)**

Nkoe – a leopard; *hlaba*
– to stab / kill; a warrior
who is brave enough to
chase and kill a leopard
or throw a spear to kill

Lehlanye

Madness; also a type of
plant *Vernonia fastigiata*

Lehumo

Fortune, wealth, riches

Leka

Try; make an attempt

Lekang

Try as a family, make an
attempt; in the plural to
show respect even
though referring to an
individual

Lekanyo

Equalise; make similar

Lekau

A gentleman, a young
man

Lekgale

A crab

Lekgala

An aloe (plant, Arabic),
grows in South Africa

Lekgotla

Court of law (social disharmony); a gathering

Lekolang

Investigate, examine, probe

Lengau

A cheetah

Lentswe (Lencoe)

The voice; the word

Lephethi (Lepheto)

The end, completion; the name signifies completion of a family thus given to last child

Lephosa

Phoso – error; to err or born due to a mistake; unplanned pregnancy

Phosa – to throw; one who throws or hurls - a thrower

Lepôgô

A cheetah

Lerumo

A spear, assegai; signifies strength

Lesetja (Lesetsa)

A spark or small ray of light

Lesiba

A feather

Lesibana

A small feather

Letsa

Call, call upon; ring

Letsapa

An opportunity, prospect;
a laborious act

Letlotlo (Letlôtlô)

Honour; could also be a
fund, possessions or
treasure

Letshwenyo

Troublesome, spiteful;
naughty

Letsie

A name of a well-known
chief of the Basotho
nation; *tsie* – a
grasshopper; could be
one who exhibits locust /
grasshopper
characteristics

Letsoalo (Letswalo)

Fear, apprehension

Leuba

Coldness accompanied
by strong winds brought
about by snow; a cold
front

Lewatle

The ocean, sea

Liale

The **L** is pronounced as
a **D**. Son of Tabane
(Pedi chief) who called
himself *Mopedi* which in
turn, gave birth to the
term Bapedi

Liemiso

Of a standing, calibre;
stature

Liepollo

Exposure; digging
deeper to disclose

M

Madikologa

Dikologa – to go round and round; the one who doesn't commit but changes their mind continuously; could also mean the crazy one or wild child

Madimo

The kings – sovereign; of higher places or supremacy; thunder

Madume

Greetings

Maepo

A place where digging takes place e.g mines; child conceived in that area

Maesela (Maisela)

Isa (v) – to take or bring to; one who delivers or brings to fruition

Magalane

Magala – red burning coal, feistiness; also *magala* - to want what others have or are having especially foodwise, salivating

Mahanna

Hana – to refuse or deny; one who is constantly refusing or in denial

Mafokane

Go foka – to annoy, pester, one who pesters;

also mean to blow away or off; the blower

Magola

Gola – to grow; the one to watch or take notice of as heading for greatness

Mahlale

Wisdom; mischief

Mahlomola

Misery, grief, sorrow

Makalang

Be surprised or delighted; enchanting or charming one

Maiphiri

Phiri – hyena; one who exhibits hyena-like characteristics

Makapane

Name of a little village in the North-west province

Makau

Gentlemen, boys

Makgaole (Mak*h*aole)

Kgaola – to break or severed; one who divides, breaks the family apart

Makgetha (Mak*h*etha)

The chooser; one who selects or a decision maker

Makgotlha

Many gatherings (court) or councils; depicts importance

Maleka

One who attempts, tries

Malekutu

The eldest of the eight sons of the Pedi chief/king, Thulare, whose reign was shortened due to poisoning

Malesela

Go lesa – to let be or leave behind; one who leaves someone behind or a starter but never completes

Maloka

Loka – fine, great; of kindness, integrity and importance

Mametsa

Metsa – to swallow; a swallower or one who loves eating

Mamphemphe

Chestnut backed Finchlark (*Eremopterix lencotis*)

Mampuru

One of Sekwati's (Pedi chief) sons who lived in Sekhukhuneland

Mangope

Washed out banks in the river; also, the name of the ex-president of Bophuthatswana (now the North-West Province)

Manaka (Dinaka)

Horns; also a stoppered flask made from horn of an ox

Masenya

The destroyer; one who ruins things and even comes between families

Masekela

Hugh Masekela, a famous South African musician

Maseko

Keen cross-examiner; an observer

Maphoto

Lumps; a very difficult character; lumpy and not easy going; controversial

Maputle

A predator (hasty ones)

Marabe

Puff-adders

Mareka

From the English Mark; second Book of the New Testament

Marema

A lumberjack or Wood cutter

Marena

Kings (historical), respected chiefs of tribes or clans; also the 11th and 12th Books of the Old Testament

Marumo

Spears, assegai, swords

Marungwana

Small spears, swords

Mathotha

One who relocates; a wanderer

Mathibela

One who hinders or restricts

Mathopa

Go thopa – to win, conquer; a conqueror

Masilo

Go sila – to grind; a place where grinding takes place; a grinder

Masole

Soldiers

Masopha

Son of the King and founder of the Basotho nation

Mateu

From the English Matthew; 1st book of the New Testament

Matlhaba

A striker; a warrior

Matlhabi

Act of striking or stabbing; stitches, pain

Matlhakanye

One who causes upheavals

Matseba

One with knowledgeable; intellectual

Matsena

One who arrives or
enters

Matshaba

A coward; one who lacks
confidence

Matshela

Tshela – to cross, one
who crosses over; also
means to jump, a
runaway

Mehlolo

Bewilderment, perplexity;
shock

Melodi

Whistles; songs, music

Mmeshake

From the English name
Meshack

Mmeshi

Short for Mmeshake,
Meshack (English name)

Mmetli

A carver, craftsman,
carpenter

Mmoti

The glorified one;
dignified one

Mmusetsi

The returner

Mmushi

A ruler, governer

Moabi

Someone who shares; a
dealer

Moagi

A builder, mason

Moathlodi

The judge

Modisa

A sheperd, a herdsman
or boy; a guard

Modisagarekwe

'A sheperd (carer)
cannot be bought' i.e one
should be honourable
and trustworthy;

Modisane

Dimunitive of *Modisa*
(herd-boy, sheperd);
A bird: Cattle Egret
(*Bubulcus ibis*)

Modise

A sheperd, a herd-boy

Modupe

A heavy rain

Moedi

A stream

Moeketsi (Mo*i*ketsi)

The one who adds or
increases; the multiplier,
proliferator

Moeletsi

An adviser

Moeno

Act of standing up or
stand up for or against;
of importance

Moetapele

A leader

Moeti

A visitor, guest

Mofati

Digger; pawing (animal)

Mofenyi

The victor, winner; triumphant one

Mofeti

A passer-by or traveller; name given usually when father is not around or didn't stay around long enough to see the child being born

Moferefere

Nuisance; trouble

Mogakanegi

Confused and indecisive person

Mogale

A brave man, a hero; also a Whitebrowed Sparrowweaver (*Plocepasser mahali*)

Mogami

One who milks (a farmer; milksman)

Moganetsi

One who opposes; an opponent

Mogapi (Mo*h*api)

The victor; an usherer or herd-boy

Mogobe

Calamity

Mogoeleng

Implore or beseech HIM

Mogome

The returner

Mogomotsi

One who comforts or sonsoles

Mogopudi

One who remembers or never forgets

Mogotsi

One who makes or lights the fire (firewood)

Mogwape

Segwapa – dried meat, biltong;

The act of drying the meat (trade name)

Mohato

A step; progress

Mohemi

A breather; one who breathes life into

Mohlabani

A warrior, a hero

Mohlalefi

A wise man, a shrewd person

Mohlahlubi

An inspector, surveyor; an accountant

Mohlaka

A vlei

Mohlala

A trail, clue; an example

Mohlapametse

Hlapa – to clean; *metse* – houses; therefore a house keeper or cleaner

Mohale (Mogale)

A brave person, a hero

Mohlobo

A race, tribe

Mohlolegi

The defeated one; a looser

Mohlophehi

A sufferer – mainly bride ill-treated by the in-laws

Mohube

Second son of Pedi chief Moukangoe

Moitiri

Self-made; entrepeneur

Mojasage

To be self sufficient; wealthy person doesn't encroach upon others

Mojalefa

Lefa – inheritance; an heir or last born child

Mojela

Eja – to eat, consume; one who consumes elsewhere but not at home; could also means to bed outside the home

Mokgaetsi (Mokaetʃi) / Mokganyetsi

A driver or conductor; one who ignites or puts lights up/on; a driver who makes things happen

Mokgaleng

Reprimand him/her; intervene

Mokgethi

Go kgetha – to choose, vote; a voter, one who nominates; a selector or determiner (importance)

Mokgethwa

The Holy one, the
chosen one

Mokhuri

One who is satisfied or
has everything the need

Mokwana

Go kwana – to get along;
one who unites people or
creates peacefullness

Mookodi

A rainbow

Mokopeng

Go kopa – to ask; ask
him (the Lord)

Mokotsi

Kotsi – danger; of
danger; dangerous;
mischievious

Mokupi

Go kopa – to ask; the
one who asks/requests

Mokwepa (Mokopa)

Black mouthed mamba
(snake)

Molahlegi

The lost one; mis-
directed

Molaka

Pepperbark tree
(Warburgia salutaris),
used to treat abdominal
pains

Molao

The law, rule

Molapo

A stream, river; name of
a Basotho chief

Molatedi

A disciple, follower

Molatelo

A follower; the successor

Molato

Debt, mistake; guilt

Moleele

The tall one

Molefe (Molef*i*)

One who pays, settles debt

Moleko

Temptation, danger, mischief; bewilderment

Molefelo

Payment

Moloi

A witch

Moloto

Go lota – to honour and respect; the honourable one; a place (village) in the Northern Province

Molotsi

One who whittles; a carpenter

Moloko

Tribe, clan

Molope

Longtailed Widow (*Euplectes progne*); it's also a Weeping Boer-Bean tree and the bark contains tannin

Molema (Molem_i_)

A farmer, agriculturalist

Monaheng

Of the land; a wanderer

Montshi

An usher; one who takes (others) out

Monyamedi

One who disappears; vanishes

Moraba

A pocket

Morafe

A tribe or nation (**morafo** – a quarry)

Morake

A house, dwelling

Morako

A wall

Moraloki

A player – in sport; an actor / actress; someone afraid of commitment

Morare

A discussion, conversation

Morekwa

The bought/purchased one

Morema (Morem_i_)

A wood cutter

Morena

The Lord; king, chief, sign of respect for an older man or the elderly

Morero

A sermon – act of discussing or preaching

Morewane

The namesake

Moroamasedile

Moroa – the son of; the son of Masedile (one left behind); son of *Masedi* (Lights) *sedile* (sun rise)

Moroamoche

Sekhukhuni's (Pedi chief) grandson; *moroa* – son of ... (Moche)

Moroba

Easy, straightforward

Morobe

A Puzzle bush (*Ehretia rigida*) – belongs to the forget-me-not family; it is used for making fishing baskets

Morobi

One who breaks or splits

Moruti

A priest, pastor; man of God

Morwa (Moroa)

Son (male child)

Morwamawoti

Son of Mawoti (the emaciated one)

Morwamotse

Son (*moroa*) of the family (*motse*); also the name of Sekhukhune's (Pedi chief) grandson who instigated the rebellion against the apartheid 'Bantu' authoritarians around 1958

Morwapelo

Son of <u>Pelo</u> (heart)

Mosala

The remainder

Mosedi

A brook, canal

Mosela

A tail

Moselantja

Dog's tail

Mosemodi

The initiator

Mosepedi

The traveller

Moshe

From the English Moses

Moshia

One who absconds

Moshoeu (Mosh*w*eu)

A white person, a person with a light skin tone

Mosimane

A boy

Mosimanegape

Another boy

Mosireletsi

A protector

Mosiuwa (Mosiu*oa*)

Go siya – to leave or let go, the abandoned one; *mosi* is also the smoke - the smoke that ...

Mosupi

A male guide or advisor

Motanyane

Go tanya – to stick to;
one who creates bonds
or keeps family together

Motabele (Motebele)

One from *Matebele* land

Mothei

One who (decides on)
names; the founder

Mothiba

One who obstructs,
hinders progress

**Mothokgwa (Mothok*o*a
/ Mothok*w*a)**

Sethokwa – a forest,
thicket or bush; the man
of/from the forest or bush

Mothopi (Moth*u*pi)

The victor, winner

Motlalepule

One who brings rain

Motlhabi

A warrior

Motodi (Mot*h*odi)

The founder; name of the
third son of the Pedi
chief, *Moroamoche*

Motsamai

One who leaves; a
traveller

Motsha

Son of *Liale* and
Tabane's (Pedi chief)
grandson

Motshoari

A care taker; a prisoner

Motsumi (Motsomi)

The hunter; a seeker

Mphaka

A knife; a sharp person

Mphato

A grade or category; an initiation lodge

Mpolokeng

Take care of me, keep me safe; also, bury me

Mpolayeng

Kill me; signifies extreme pain maybe due to a difficult birth

Mpshe

An ostrich

Nape

Then or ought to; from Spanish *Napier* meaning 'of the city' *Neper*

Nare

Buffallo

Nepo

Appropriate; suitable

Ngako

House (household)

Ngwako (Ngoako)

House, dwelling, home

Nkagiseng (Nkaiseng)

Help me build ...a family; be neighbourly, friendly, welcoming

Nkagisane

Neighbourliness, hospitality

Nko

A nose

Nkoe (Nkwe)

A tiger (a praise name)

Nku

A sheep (praise name)

Nkweseng

Let me experience it; a taster

Noko

A porcupine (praise name); symbolises a good omen and is a totem of the Maroteng people (Pedi)

Nonê

Blesbuck (praise name)

Nong

A vulture (praise name)

Ntja

A dog (praise name)

Ntshimane

A boy

Ntsu

An eagle [black eagle] – *Aquila verreauxii*

Nyakanyaka

Nyaka – to seek; one who's always seeking or unsatisfied; a huntsman

Nyako

Search, seek

Oabile

God has shared or bequeathed

Obakeng

Praise Him (the Lord)

Oetse (Weetse)

He has made it happen

Okgopotse

HE has remembered you

Olaotse

HE has commanded

Onkgopetse

HE has asked of me

Onkgopotse

HE has remembered me

Oteng

He (a boy) is present or has been born

Otlantheng

'What could HE say to me?' What response would he give me?

Otumiso

HE is gracious; praiseworthy

Oupa

Grandfather; to honour the parents

Oupanyana

Little grandfather, in honour of the grandfather

P

Pakeng

Where one testifies
(could be court);
testimony

Paki

Short form of *Pakiso*
(witness, evidence)

Pakiso

Evidence, testimony

Paledi

Go pala – unsolvable or
hard to decipher; difficult,
indeterminate

Papetso

Advertise, announce;
playfull

Papiki

Papa – father (from
Afrikaans), small father -
to honour parent's father

Paseka

Easter, one born on
Easter

Pelo

Heart; signifies love

Pêolwane

A swallow or a swift
(*Apus sp*)

Peu (Peo)

Seed

Phaahla

A gap, crack; also a
forehead

Phahamo

Elevation; renown

Phala

An antelope

Phalafala

A war horn - often sounded to gather the initiates who are to present for their first *Koma* (initiation) session

Phalima (Phad̵ima)

To shine; stand out

Phalwane

Phala – antelope, a small antelope; also a flute or horn - a small flute

Phatudi

Ex-president of Lebowa now, Northern Province

Pheeha

To deny, denial

Pheehello

Determination, perserverance

Pheko

A cure, a remedy

Phetedi

Repetition or follow up; also third son of chief Thulare who was killed by the Matebele people

Phetisi

Completeness; ending, conclusion

Phiri

Hyena (praise name), person to exhibit hyena-like characteristics

Phokeng

A little town in the North-West province near to Rustenburg; a place of dew

Phokwana (Phokoana)

A young billy-goat

Pholo

An ox; depicts strength

Phuthego

Congregate (a congregation); coming together

Phuti

Duiker

Pilwane

Dimunitive of Pilo (harvest?)

Piti

From the Afrikaans name *Piet* (Peter) – Latin for 'rock' or 'stone'

Pitsi

Zebra (Horse)

Pitso

A calling, meeting

Polomashwashe

Alligator; short form *Polo*

Pome

To shave off – one who lets go of …;

Also, short form for *Phomelello* – success, accomplishment

Pontsho

Show, exhibition; proof

Potso

A question

Puo

Talk, language, gossip

Puso

Rule, governance

Pule (Pula)

Of rain; rain

R

Rabotsipa

Botsipa – prickly, a very thorny character; also to honour a certain Mr. Botsipa - influential in person's life

Raditshetlhwana (Raditshêhloane)

Tshêhlô – thorn; devil's thorn *(Tribulus terrestris L.); Tshetlhwana* – a small thorn 'man of thorns' – maybe a thorny character

Rakau

Kau – short for *Lekau* (a gentleman or a boy), father of *Kau*; also in honour of Mr. Kau (surname) or a male relative

Rakgolane

Rakgolo – grandfather, a small grandfather; name used to honour the parent's male grandparents

Rakomane

Koma - initiation ceremony; a boy named after a male in charge of *koma*; in honour of Mr. Komane (surname) who may have been a great help or influence to the family

Rakotse

One prone to accidents, danger

Raleiye

From the English Rowley; also, *eiye* (onions) could be trade related

Ramaboya

Maboya – fur, feathers; one who deals with fur or feathers (trade name)

Ramalesela

Go lesa – to let be, leave behind, incomplete; *Malesela* – one who doesn't complete or finish anything; to hounour Mr. Malesela

Ramano

Mano – ideas, creativity; one with ideas or plans

Ramasela

Masela – material; a tailor or designer (trade name)

Ramatjato

Matjato – lively, sprightly; one with agility

Ramatla

Matla – strength; the strong one; a hero

Ramebele

Mebele – bodies (upper body); a well built man - shows strength

Ramoabi

Go aba (v) – to share; honouring a male relative called <u>Moabi</u> (a dealer, one who shares)

Ramohu

Mohu – a dead person; a child named after recent death of a relative whose name cannot be used

Ramolokwane

Moloko – a nation; *molokwane* – a small nation or tribe; head of a small tribe or nation

Ramona

Mona – envy, jealousy; an envious person

Ramoshoeu

Moshoeu – a Caucasian or white person' also one with a light skin tone; father of <u>Moshoeu</u> or in honour of Mr.<u>Mosheou</u>

Rantlopi

Tlopa – to choose; honouring male relative called <u>Ntlopi</u> (one who self- elects)

Rantwa

Ntwa - a fight; a fighter, one who is easily angered and ready for altercation

Rapata

Pata – a road, way; a traveller; one who enjoys going out (sociable), a socialite; a trade name

Rasekgotla

Kgotla – a court; honouring a male relative called Sekgotla (of the court)

Ramolwetsi

One who's sickly; ill health

Ratau

Father of Tau (lion)

Ratiro

Tiro – work; a worker or a workman

Ratlhogo

Hlogo – a head; one with a large head (physical attribute); one to leader

Ratsebo

One full of knowledge (*tsebo*)

Ratshidi

Ditshidi – that which is alive or the living; *Ditshidi* – a sour plum (*Ximenia caffra*) bush; to honour father of Tshidi (a girl's name, short for *Matshidiso* - condolences)

Ratshilo

A grinder; a harvester or a farmer

S

Sathakge

Thekga – to support; a pillar

Seabelo

A share, inheritance

Seakge

That's which holds together

Seaparo

Garment, clothing; that which covers or shields; the protector

Sebaka

Chance, opportunity; a cause

Sebata

Beast

Sebetlane

A carver; creator

Sebolaishi

That which gets one into tight corners or trouble

Sebêsô (Sebes*h*o)

Domestic hearth of the Pedi people

Sechaba (Set*j*haba)

The nation

Sediba

A spring (of water)

Seemo

Stature

Sefako

Hail

Segôdi

A Steppe Buzzard
(*Buteo buteo*); that which
grows or develops

Sehlabane

A warrior

Sehlake

In or of poverty

Sehlolo

The victor

Sekwati

Lekwati – a bark of a tree
therefore a protector;
one of Thulare's sons
who established his
kingdom in Phiring

Selalankwe

One who traps or hunts
tigers; a warrior

Sekata

A guard (English word)

Sekatelane

Brown throated Martin
[African sand Martin]
(*Riparia paludicola*)

Sekgwane

Sekgwa – a forest; a little
forest

**Sekhukhune
(Sekukuni)**

Go khukhuna – to go
about without being
seeing; one who hides or
operates underhandedly;
very ambiguous and
untrustworthy person;
one of the two sons of
the Pedi chief, Sekwati,
who was the heir to the
throne

Sekoba

That which bends,
weaves; the repellant

Sekwala

A concealer; that which
covers up (like a lid); one
who is capable of
completing or finalising
tasks

Selepe

An axe

Sello

A cry, weeping, wailing

Selope

A fishing rod

Semenya

Imploring, beseeching

Sepedi

Northern Sotho
(language of Bapedi)

Seporo

Railway lines

Serame

Cold, frost

Serero

A sermon; to preach

Seretse

Mud, plaster; name of
the ex-president of
Botswana, Seretse
Kgama

Seriti

Stature, of standing, of
importance; commands
respect and is feared

Setumo

Popularity, reputation

Shimane

Boy, boyhood

Sesinyi

One who destroys, is
destructive; causes
problems leading to
disharmony

Setene

From the Afrikaans
'*Steyn*' probably to
honour that person

Sethele

Named after; namesake

Serobe

That which is broken,
destroyed

Serobele

House sparrow (*Passer
domesticus*)

Serokolo

Pied Barbet (*Lybius
leucomelas*)

T

Taelo

A command, an order or instruction

Tâle

Masked Weaver (*Ploceus velatus*)

Taole

A composition; bones used by traditional doctors to foresee

Taolo

Control, regulation, commandment

Taoloetsile

Order has come; we've received the commandment

Tatolo

Denial

Tau

A lion (a praise name); a king; also a tribal fireplace of the Pedi people

Tefo

A reward, payment

Teko

Test, analysis

Thaba

A mountain; be happy, grateful

Thabane

A small mountain or a hill

Thabeng

Of the mountains; pet form *Thabe*

Thabiso

Happiness, joy, celebration

Thaga

Spectacled Weaver (Ploceus ocularis)

Thakane

Thaka – a peer, friend, play mate; small friend

Thapang

To get wet; a child born on the day when family is paying tribute to the ancestors whereby wetting the ground with alcohol is part of the celebration

Thapedi

Appeal

Thebe

Shield

Theko

Forktailed Drongo (*Dicrurus adsimilis*)

Thero

Sermon

Thipana

Medicine man who deals with initiation (circumcisions); also a small knife/blade

Thipe

An antelope

Thobela

A Sotho greeting (hello);
also name of a famous
Bakgatla chief

Thulakome

Kori Bustard (*Ardeotis
kori*)

Tiro

An act, deed, a job

Tiego

Delay; one who is
delayed

Tjale

A throw, blanket; a
protector

Tladi

Thunder (storm)

Tlalane

Filled up, fulfillment;
impressionable

Tlhabane (*H*labane)

Battle

Tlou

An elephant (one with
great presence)

Tokollo

Freedom; virtuous,
righteousness

Tseko (T*sh*eko)

Interrogation; prosecutor

Tsela

Path (way); one with
direction

Tshêhlô

Devil's thorn (*Tribulus terrestris L.*) believed to cause 'Geeldikkop disease' among small stock

Tshepe

Springbuck

Tshetlho

Greater Honeyguide (*Indicator indicator*)

Tshilwane

Tshilo – grinder; small act of grinding

Tshipi

A bell; steel; a hard person

Tshirelo

Protection

Tshwene (Chuene)

Baboon (a praise name)

Tsie

Locust, grasshopper

Tsietsi

Distress, trouble, predicament

Tsoso

A revival, resurrection

Tshukudu

A black rhinoceros (poetic name signifying physical attributes)

BRIDAL NAMES (DENOTING MOTHER OF SO-AND-SO)

In celebrating matrimony, the in-laws would give the bride a marital name (bridal name) by which the husband is also expected to call her. This name should incorporate the name that the in-laws expect or wish her (the daughter-in-law) to give to her first child and which also amplifes their wish for a specific gender. Sometimes bridal names can be harsher and may only be done once she has produced a child. Should she fail the family and not deliver a grandchild, the name will definitely depict that sentiment.

Machuene

Mother of Chuene – (a monkey)

Magomang

"Whose mother are you?" A very cruel bride name, one given to a bride who hasn't manged to have child; the barren one

Maiphiri

Mother of Phiri (hyena) but possibly misspelt

Makanyane (Makonyane)

Mother of a Konyana (lamb)

Makgomo

Mother of Kgomo (cow, cattle, dowry)

Makgwale

Mother of Kgwale (Natal Francolin)

Makoena (Makwena)

Mother of Koena (a crocodile)

Malehlogonolo

Mother of Lehlogonolo (blessing, luck)

Malehumo

Mother of Lehumo (wealth)

Malekau

Mother of Lekau (boy, gentleman); family wish to have grandsons

Malesiba

Mother of Lesiba (a feather)

152

Maletsa

Mother of Letsa (bush buck)

Mamaki

Mother of Maki (from Dimakatso, a marvel)

Mamatome

Mother of Matome (Matthew – English)

Mamodikwe

Mother of Modikwe (a smooth black lizard)

Mamodimo

Mother of Modimo (a king; GOD)

Mamodise

Mother of Modise (sheperd)

Mamodupi (Mamodupe)

Mother of Modupe (heavy rain)

Mamohau

Mother of Mohau (mercy; kind-hearted)

Mamohlabane

Mother of Mohlabane (a warrior)

Mamoiketsi (Mamoeketsi)

Mother of Moeketsi (one who adds or increases the family)

Mamokete

Mother of Mokete (celebration)

Mamoloko

Mother of a Moloko
(tribe, nation)

Mamonye

Mother of Monye (one,
single); alone or unable
to have more children

Mamorare

Mother of Morare (a
discussion)

Mamorena

Mother of Morena (the
Lord, King, chief); one of
good standing in the
community

Mamotshe (Mamoše)

Mother of Motshe
(Moses – English)

Mamoyagae

Mother of Moyagae (one
who returns home;
returning after divorce)

Mampokeng

Go poka – when the
dead visit the living
(ghostly appearance);
mother of Mpokeng (one
who sees ghosts or is in
communication with the
ancestors); one who's
delusional

Mampshe

Mother of Mpshe
(ostrich)

Mampshedi

Mother of Mpshedi
(female ostrich)

Mampusane

Puso – governing, ruling; mother of Mpusane (a ruler or who's in control)

Manake

Nake – pet form for Nakedi (a pole cat),

Nnake – a sibling, mother of my sibling or close relative who grew up together

Manare

Mothe of Nare (wildebeest – praise name)

Mangakane

Mother of Ngakane (a small doctor)

Manku

Mother of Nku (sheep – praise name)

Manose

Mother of Osi (one; one offspring)

Mantho

Mother of something (*Ntho* – a thing); after pregnancies resulting in still births

Mantsadi

Mother of girls (family wishing to have granddaughters)

Mantsu

Mother of Ntsu (an eagle – praise name)

Mapêo

Mother of Pêo (a
swallow); believed that
the namesake might fly
away, disappear

Mapeu

Mother of Peu (a seed,
offspring)

Maphuti

Mother of Phuti (duiker)

Mapitso

Mother of Pitso (a
calling, vocation)

Masello

Mother of Sello (wailing,
cries, tears)

Maserame

Mother of Serame (cold,
winter, frost)

Maseretse

Mother of Seretse (mud);
Seretse Kgama was the
president of Botswana

Mathabiso

Mother of Thabiso
(happiness)

Mathabo

Mother of Thabo
(happiness, delight)

Mathapelo

Mother of Thapelo
(prayer)

Mathato

Mother of Thato (will,
wish)

Mathebe

Mother of Thebe (a
shield)

Mathobela

Mother of Thobela
(greetings, welcome)

Matlale

Mother of Tlale
(fulfilment; contented)

Matlogile

Mother of Tlogile (one
who's left/departed)

Matloo

Mother of Tloo (a beast)

Matlou

Mother of Tlou (an
elephant)

Matsatsi

Mother of Tsatsi
(sunshine)

Matsekiso

Mother of Tsekiso (of the
court, interrogation)

Matselane

Mother of Tselane (a
small path)

Matshelane

Mother of Tshelane (a
small life)

Matshego

Mother of Tshego short
for Tshegofatso
(blessings)

Matsheko

Mother of Tsheko (court
of law, a lawyer or judge)

Matshepe

Mother of Tshepe (a
springbok)

Matshepo

Mother of Tshepo (Hope)

Matshwene

Mother of Tshwene
(Monkey, ape)

Matsie

Mother of Tsie (locust,
grasshopper)

Matsietsi

Mother of Tsietsi
(trouble, distress)

Mmabontle

Mother of Bontle
(beauty)

Mmabosi (Mmabusi)

Mother of Bosi (*busa* – to
ruler, a ruler)

Mmaditaba

Mother of Ditaba (news)

Mmakafiri

Mother of Kafiri (from the
Afrikaans *Kaffir*, which is
a derogatory word used
during apartheid to refer
to a black person); it is
also a family of plants –
kaffir beans (*Vigna
sinensis*), kaffir melons
(*Citrus vulgaris* sp.)

Mmakatse

Mother of Katse (cat –
praise name)

Mmakgabo

Mother of Kgabo
(monkey)

Mmakgoshi (Mmakgosi)

Mother of a Kgoshi (king)

Mmakhudu

Mother of Khudu (tortoise)

Mmakhumo

Mother of Khumo (wealth); one who is wealthy

Mmakoloi

Mother of Koloi (a vehicle)

Mmakwena

Mother of Kwena (crocodile)

Mmalego

Mother of Lego (death); or wooden spoon

Mmalekgowa

Mother of Lekgowa (a white person)

Mmalephallo

Mother of Lephallo (one who is cleverer than the peers)

Mmalerato (Malerato)

Mother of Lerato (Love, affection)

Mmaletsatsi

Mother of Letsatsi (the sun)

Mmalodi

Mother of Lodi, short for *Mologadi* (a thinker and creative one)

Mmamaredi

Mother of Maredi
(slippery; smooth
operator); wife of Mr.
Maredi (surname)

Mmamasenya

Mother of Masenya (the
destroyer)

Mmamokete

Mother of Mokete
(celebration)

Mmamokgethwa

Mother of Mokgethwa
(the Holy one; the
chosen one)

Mmamorati

Mother of Morati (one
who loves or desires)

Mmamose

Mother of Mose (Moses
– Hebrew for 'saved')

Mmamushi

Mother of Mushi (the
ruler, governor)

Mmamutla

Mother of Mutla (rabbit)

Mmakedi

Mother of Kedi, short for
Kediso (enlightenment)

Mmalehu

Mother of Lehu (death);
one born of death of after
death of family member;
all pregnancies end as
stillbirth

Mmanakedi

Mother of Nakedi (Pole
cat)

Mmankedi

Mother of Nkedi, short
for *Dikeledi* (tears)

Mmanku

Mother of Nku (sheep) or
Blackcollared Barbet

Mmanoko

Mother of Noko
(porcupine)

Mmantsatsi

Mother of Ntsatsi,
dimunitive of *Letsatsi*
(the sun)

Mmapaseka

Mother of Paseka
(Easter; born on Easter)

Mmapelo

Mother of Pelo (heart)

Mmaphala

Mother of Phala
(antelope, horn, flute)

Mmapitso

Mother of Pitso (a
calling, vocation)

Mmapula

Mother of Pula (rain)

Mmasape

Mother of Sape (taken
from the German *Sepp*,
a form of Joseph
meaning 'God will
increase')

Mmasello

Mother of Sello (a cry;
cries, weeping)

Mmasepala

Mother of Sepala (a non-achiever or unsuccessful person); could be a trade name - a council, government

Mmasepeke

Mother of Sepeke (from the English word 'speaker')

Mmasetshaba

Mother of Setshaba (the nation)

Mmashela

Mother of Shela; could be from the English word *shell* meaning 'armour'; also, a variation of *Sheila* (Irish Cecilia) meaning 'dim-sighted'

Mmathapelo

Mother of Thapelo (prayer)

Mmatlou

Mother of Tlou (an elephant)

Mmatoka

Mother of Toka (justice)

Mmatsego

Mother of Tsego, short for *Tsegofatso* (blessing)

Mmatshadi

Mother of Tshadi (a female, lady)

Mmatsheko

Mother of Tsheko (court of law)

Mmatsheo

Mother of Tsheo, short
for *Tshegofatso*
(blessing)

Mmatshepo

Mother of Tshepo
(hope); one who's
hopeful

Mmatshepe

Mother of Tshepe (a
springbok)

Mmatshoke

Mother of Tshoke
(perserverance)

NAMES ACKNOWLEDGING GOD

Among the Sotho-speaking tribes, it is common to find names that express gratitude towards God. This is to enforce the belief that children are indeed considered a blessing and a gift from God *Modimo*. Also, the ancestors *Badimo* are still respected and feared and therefore honoured. These names usually begin with the letter **O** or the letter is embedded within the name. Alternatively, the names will have some religious connotation.

A

Aobakwe

Let HIM be praised

B

Bakang

Praise the Lord; adore,
worship and commend
HIM

Bokang

Praise, adore and
commend HIM

Botang

Glorify, worship the Lord

D

Diketso

God's deeds, work,
actions

Dithoriso

Rorisa (v) – worship;
relentless worshipping

G

Garaipha

Ipha – to adorn oneself;
g*ara* – we didn't. We
haven't bequeathed or
bestowed upon
ourselves i.e God has

Goitseone

Only HE knows

K

Kaone

With or about HIM (God)

Kedumetse

I have believed or
accepted

165

Keodirelang

What could I do for God?

Keolebogile

I've thanked HIM

Keorapetse

I've prayed to... GOD

Keotshepile

I trust in HIM

Kesaobaka

I'm still praising HIM

◐

Oabile

HE has shared or bequeathed

Oarabile

HE has answered our prayers

Obakeng

Praise HIM

Obohlale (Obot/hale)

HE is wise indeed

Odirile

HE has made it possible or to happen

Ofentse

HE is victorious

Ofile

He has given, bequeathed

Ogona

HE is present or is in existence

Oitseone

Only HE knows

166

Okgopetswe

He has been asked or prayed to

Olebogeng

Thank HIM; be grateful to HIM

Olethabo

HE is joy, happiness

Omphile

HE has given or blessed me

Onkarabetse

HE has answered me or my prayers

Olaotse

HE has commanded

Omatla

HE is powerful

Omolemo

God is merciful

Omphemetse

HE has allowed it to occur

Omphile

HE has given to me

Omphileone

He gave him/her to me

Oneile

HE has given

Onkatlile

Atla (v) – to kiss; HE has embraced me (a sign of acceptance)

Onkgopetse

Kopa (v) – to ask; HE has asked of me

Onkgopotse

Gopola – to remember; HE has remembered me (Remembrance)

Onthatile

HE has showered (shown) me with love

Orapeleng

Rapela – to pray; pray to HIM

Oratile

HE has so loved or wished it

Oratiloe (Oratilwe)

HE is loved

Ontiretse

Tiro – deed, work; HE has come through for me

Orebabaletse

HE has protected us

Oreteng

Praise HIM

Ororiseng

Praise HIM

Oteng

HE is present; God does exist

Othabo

HE is happiness

Otsile

HE has come

Otlotleng

Honour HIM; praise HIM

Otumiso

HE is gracious

Owame

HE is mine; HE is my Lord

R

Reauboka

We praise HIM

Reaotlotla

We praise HIM

Rebotile

We have glorified, worshipped HIM

Rorisang

Praise, honour HIM

T

Thatoyaone

God's will

Tumiso (Tumis*ho* / Tumis*hi*)

Praise (to HIM)

Tumisang

Praise HIM

NAMES SIGNIFYING ACCEPTANCE

A

Amogelang

Receive, accept (be receptive)

K

Kamogelo

Acceptance, approval, reception

Kamogetso

Embrace, approved; welcome,

Keamogetse

I've received, accepted

Keamogetswe (Keamogetsoe)

I've been well received, embraced, accepted

Kefiloe (Kefilwe)

I've been given, bequeathed

Kefuoe

I've been given, bequeathed

O

Oamogetswe

He/she (the baby) has
been well received,
accepted

Omphile

I have been given (by
HIM)

Oneile

HE has given

R

**Reabetsoe
(Reabetswe)**

We've inherited, been
given, bequeathed

Refilwe (Refiloe)

We've been given,
blessed

Reneilwe

We've been blessed,
bequeathed

**Reneetsoe
(Reneetswe)**

We've been given,
blessed

NAMES DENOTING GIFTS

D

Dimpho

Gifts, offerings

Dineo

Gifts

E

Eneiloe (Eneilwe)

It's been given, bequeathed

K

Kabelo

One's share/quota; inheritance;

Kabo

A share

Karolo

A division, a section, a part (n)

Keboabetswe

It's been bequeathed upon me, given to me

Keabetswe (Keabetsoe)

It's been given tom me (my share)

Kefiloe (Kefilwe)

I've been given

L

Lefilwe

You've been given;
allocated

Leoneetsoe

You've been given,
blessed

Lesebo

A gift from the ancestors

M

Mpho

A gift

Mphonyana

A small gift

N

Neo

A gift; an offering

NAMES DENOTING LOVE

B

Banthata

I am loved

Baratang

Those who love;
admirers

D

Dithato

Wishes, love, desire

K

Keratile

I've loved, wished

L

Lerato (Lorato)

Love, affection;
admiration

N

Nthateng

Love and adore me

O

Olerato

HE is love

Oratile

HE has loved

R

Rategile

Beloved, loved

Ratile

Loved, affedctionate

NAMES SIGNIFYING GRATEFULNESS

D

Ditebogo

Gratitute, gratefulness, appreciation

K

Kefilwe (Kefiloe / Kef*uo*e)

I've been given. I've been blessed

Kelebogile

I'm grateful, thankful

Kelefiwe

I've been rewarded; awarded

L

Leboga (*s*)

Be thankful

Lebogang (*pl*)

Be grateful, thankful

Lebogile

Grateful

M

Malebo

Gratitute, thanks

Molebogeng

Thank HIM; give thanks to HIM

T

Tebogo

Thanks, gratitute

Tshegofatso

A blessing

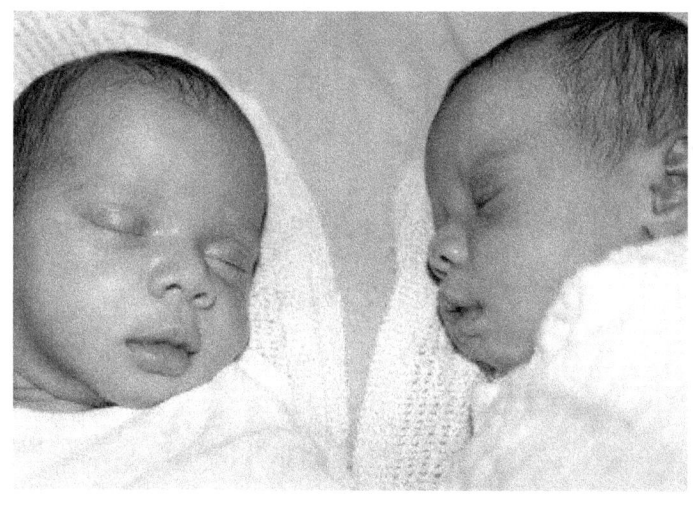

NAMES DENOTING HAPPINESS

B

Bathabile

They're joyous, happy

Boitumelo

Joy, Happiness

D

Dithabo

Magnified excitement, joys

Dithabong

A place of joy; in/of happiness

Ditshego

Laughter, happiness

I

Itumeleng

Be happy, content, delighted

K

Keitumetse

I am happy

Kethabile

I am happy

Kethabo

T'is happiness

L

Lethabo

Happiness

M

Mathabo (g)

The happy one;
countless happiness;
also mother of <u>Thabo</u>
(happiness)

N

Nthabeleng

Be happy for me; rejoice
with me

Nthabiseng

Make me happy

Nthateng

Love and adore me

O

Olethabo

HE is happiness

Othabo

HE is happiness

Othabile

He/she is joyful, happy

R

Reitumetse

We are happy, joyous

Rethabile

We are happy, joyous

T

Thaba (s)

Be happy

Thabang (*pl*)

Rejoice, be happy

Thabelo

Happiness

Thabeng

Where there's joy

Thabile

Happy, happiness

Thabiso

Happiness, joy,
celebration

Thabo

Joy

Thakgatso

Happiness

R

Rethabile

We are joyous

W

Wathabo

Of happiness

NAMES SIGNIFYING HOPE

B

Boitshepo

Hopefulness

D

Ditshepo

Lots of hope

Ditshepiso

Hopefulness

K

Ketshepile

I have hoped or trusted in ... (Lord)

Ketshepo

It (he/she) is hope

Kholofelo (*Holofelo*)

Hope

T

Tshepang

Be hopefull

Tshepiso

Promise, hope

Tshepo

Hope

Tshepong

Where hope exists

Tsholofelo

Hope

181

NAMES SIGNIFYING PEACE AND CALM

B

Boikhutso

A peaceful, restful place

Bollele

Gentleness

Bonolo

Gentle (soul); ease, calm

D

Dikhutso

Lots of rest, peace; tranquillity

Dikhutsong

Place of rest or a restful place

K

Kagiso

Peace, harmony, serenity

Kgotso (Khotso)

Peace, calm, serenity

Khutsang

Be at peace

Khutso

Rest, peace

P

Phomolo

Rest, peace

Phomolong

A place of rest, peace

T

Tholang

Quiten, calm down

Tidimallo

Quietness, serenity

Tidimatso

Silence, quietness

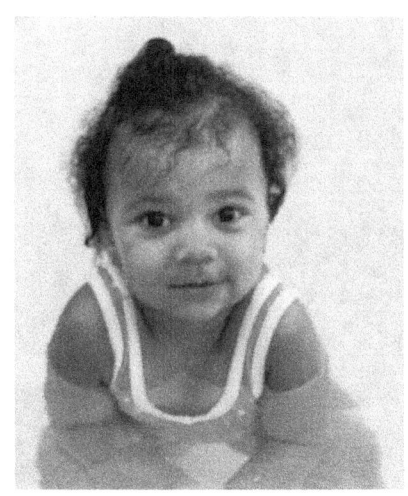

NAMES DENOTING PRIDE

B

Boikgantso

Pride; vanity

Boipelo

Self-pride, dignity, self-respect

I

Ikgantseng

Be proud, pleased; have pride

Ipeleng

Be proud, pleased

K

Kganyago

One who shines, excels

Kgantso

Pride; pleasure

M

Moipone

An arrogant, aloof person; self-admirer

P

Phalima

To stand out, shine

S

Seipone

One who is vain, conceited

NAMES DENOTING WISDOM

B

Bohlale (Bot/hale)

Wisdom, insight

Baatseba

K

Kediso

Enlightenment;
clarification (pertaining to
insight, knowledge or
awareness)

Keitso (Kitso)

Knowledge

Kelello

Knowledgeable,
intelligence; able to think

Keletso

Advice

Kitso

Knowledge

M

Matseba

One with knowledge; an
intellectual

Matsebo (g)

One with knowledge; an
intellectual

O

Obohlale (Obot/hale)

HE is wise

R

Ratsebo (*b*)

One with knowledge

S

Seeletso

That which gives
guidance; advice

Setsibi

An intellectual; one with
knowledge or with
information

T

Tsebile

Known; knowledgeable

Tsebo

Knowledge

Tsebong

In the know; of
knowledge

W

Watsebo

One with knowledge

NAMES INDICATING A WISH FOR MORE CHILDREN

A

Ata

Multiply, increase

Atang

Multiply; grow as a family

Atisang

Add, increase

D

Dieketseng

Multiply, extend

Dioketso

Expansion, amplification

K

Katafalo

The act of multiplying; growth

Katiso

Multiplication, enlargement

Keketso

Increament, amplification

Kgodiso

Growth, development, increament

Kgodisho

Growth, development

Kgudišo (Kgudisho)

Growth, development; harvest

Koketso

Addition

L

Leago

A building or shell of a building; given to second kids with hope for a third

M

Moeketsi (Moiketsi)

One who adds to the family; increases, multiplies

Motheo

A foundation, the beginning of a family

O

Oageng

Build the family, procreate

1

2

5

4

3

NAMES INDICATING SUCCESS/ FORTUNE

A

Atlegang

Prosper, flourish; be successful

Aganang

Aga (v) – to build; help each other develop, prosper; come together

Agang

Aga (v) – to build; develop, increase

Agisegang

Let there be growth, prosperity among you

B

Bathopi

Victors, conquerors; winners

F

Fenyang

Be victorious

K

Katlego

Success, fruitfulness

Katliso

Accomplishments, victory

Kedirile

I've conquered, accomplished

Kefentse

I've succeeded, triumphed

Kehumile

I am wealthy, affluent

Khumo

Wealth

L

Lefentse (Refentse - *pl*)

You've triumphed, conquered; overcome

Lehumo

Wealth, fortune

M

Mofenyi

The victor; triumphant

Mohapi

The victor

Muhluri

Victorious

Mothupi (Mothopi)

The victor, winner

Ofentse

He/she is victorious

Phenyo

Victory

NAMES DENOTING DEFEAT / MISFORTUNE

B

Bafedile

They're defeated, they've been obliterated; they are all gone

Bahlolegile

They've been defeated

K

Kebusitswe

I've been returned, brought back from in-laws

Kedibone

I've seen it all; I've suffered enough

Kediemetse

I've persevered; survived tough/bad times

Kelekilwe

I've been challenged, tested

Kenosi

I am alone, lonesome; often used when all family members have passed on

Keutlwile

I've persevered, had experienced enough ill-treatment

Kgathatso

Bothersome,
exasperating

M

Mashiko

Mother of nothing
(barren)

Mohlophehi

One who suffers or is
born into suffering even
misfortune

P

Phehello

Perserverance

T

Thloriso

Abuse; ill-treatment

Tsietsi

Distress, trouble

NAMES HONOURING

MOTHER'S

MALE RELATIVES

In order to honour maternal uncles or mother's male relatives, Bapedi (northern Sothos) often formulate girl names by attaching the prefix *Ra* which means 'father', to nouns or verbs. Surnames in particular, of people who have had a great influence in the parent's or the couple's lives, are used. These names sound masculine but are generally acceptable as female names and appreciated for their uniqueness.

R

Ramadimetsa

(Ramadimetʃa)

Honouring a male
relative called
Madimetsa (*madi –*
blood; *metsa* - swallow);
signifies strength

Ramadiwe

Honouring male relative
called Madiwe
(surname); that which
falls

Ramahatsane

Honouring male relative
called Mahatsane (*hatsa*
– to spread/spray, one
who spreads)

Ramaila

Honouring male relative
called Maila; (*ila* – to
react badly to certain
substances/foods;
allergic one

Ramaisela

Honouring male relative
called Maisela (*isa* – to
bring or take); one who
delivers or brings to
fruition

Ramalesela

Honouring male relative
called Malesela (*go lesa*
– to let be or leave
behind); one who starts
but never completes
tasks

Ramaredi

Honouring male relative
called Maredi (surname)
- namesake; slippery

Ramasela

Honouring male relative
called Masela (*go sela* –
to pick up; one who picks
up); *Masela* – material -
a tailor or designer (trade
name)

Ramasere

Honouring male relative
called Masere (a shield,
protector)

Ramasilele

Honouring male relative
called Masilele (one who
grinds or works with
grinders)

Ramatitsane

Honouring male relative
called Matitsane
(surname)

Ramatsabane

Honouring male relative
called Matsabane
(surname)

Ramatseba

Honouring male relative
called *Matseba*
(knowledgeable one)

Ramatsimela

Honouring male relative
called Matsimela
(surname)

Ramatsobane

Honouring male relative
called Matsobane
(matsoba – flowers)

Ramokone (Kone)

Honouring male relative called <u>Mokone</u> (of the north)

Ramolokwane

Honouring male relative called <u>Molokwane</u> (a small nation, tribe)

Ramolwetsi

Honouring male relative called <u>Molwetsi</u> (a sick person, patient)

Ramosele

Honouring male relative called <u>Mosele</u> (a tail)

Ramoshoeu

Honouring male relative called <u>Moshoeu</u> (a white person or one with a light skin tone)

Rankaelang

Honouring male relative called <u>Nkaelang</u> (guidance)

Rapaledi

Honouring male relative called <u>Paledi</u> (unsuccessful, difficult)

Rapulana

Honouring male relative called <u>Pule</u> (from *Pula* - mild rain)

NAMES WITH UNKNOWN MEANINGS

Unfortunately, it was impossible to find translations to all the names recorded but I sure hope that someone out there would know one or even more of the names listed below. Some are surnames, others *Direto* (poetic names) while others are very common but sadly no one seemed to know their meanings. Please speak to grandparents as they are more likely to know their meanings or more so, the root thereof. It would be highly appreciated if you could get in touch with the author in order to complete and update this list. Thanking you in advance.

Boreadi	Legaiwa	Mapoyi
Boshisi	Legaletloane	Maribane
Chikane	Lehudu	Masarele
Chiloane	Mabore	Masetha
Chipane	Mamatime	Masethele
Dikwapi	Mamoneke	Masupse
Ditsepu	Mamongau	Matete
Fanyane	Mamoteme	Mathulwe
Ganyane	Mamothe	Matiki
Hlapsadi	Mampidi	Matila
Hunadi	Mampupu	Matimane
Kanyane	Manche	Matipane
Kapari	Mangatsila	Matjiane
Kgabiri	Mantikana	Matlewa
Kgabjelane	Manti	Matolane
Kgorudi	Maphiki	Matseitsi

Matseke	Mokhine	Mphahlele
Matshipo	Mokhoka	Mphaladi
Matsiri	Mokwape	Mphapisane
Matsobane	Mollale (Lali)	Mphele (Mphela)
Mautla (m)	Mologadi	Maredi
Moale	Mongwai	Maropeng
Moalosi	Moswaila	Ngwahakhwethe
Modikwe	Motheba	
Modipane	Moshibudi	Nanishi
Modipe	Mothobi	Napsadi (S)
Moditji	Motsepe	Nchote
Moerane	Motsiri	Ngwaketse
Mogoshadi	Mpala	Nkgebele
Mogotle	Mpape	Nkgoba
Mokalaba	Mpetle	Nthakwana
Mokgalaka	Mpetoane	Nthokgo

Ntlakana	Pogane	Seokane
Ntsako	Seale	Serupa
Padimole	Sebaratlane	Thakalakalane
Phakale	Sebubudi	
Phalaga	Seeke	Thamage
Phaladi	Sefularo	Thulwe
Phalatse	Sejamodula	Tsako
Phaswane	Senthaolele	

REFERENCES

Grobler GM (1991).The Concise Trilingual Pocket Dictionary – English, Northern Sotho, Afrikaans. AD Donker Publisher.

Le Roux JC (1991). The Concise Trilingual Pocket Dictionary – English, Tswana, Afrikaans AD Donker Publisher.

Maclean GL (1985). Roberts Birds of Southern Africa. 5th Edition. John Voelcker Bird Book Fund, Cape Town.

Magubane P (1998). Vanishing Cultures of South Africa – changing customs in a changing world. The Pedi: pg 124-137. Struik Publishers (Pty) Ltd.

Moeketsi RH (1991). The Concise Trilingual Pocket Dictionary – English, Southern Sotho, Afrikaans AD Donker Publisher.

Quin PJ (1959). Foods and feeding Habits of the Pedi. BSc (Agric), MSc, DSc, PhD. Witwatersrand University Press, Johannesburg.

Shakespeare W (2005). Romeo and Juliet: Act II, Scene ii, line 43. Oxford University Press edition, Rona Gill.

Venter F and Venter J-A (1996). Making the most of indigenous trees. Briza Publications.

Wilken P - translated by B. Khotseng- (1994). Understanding everyday Sesotho: A vocabulary and reference book. Maskew Miller Longman (Pty).

ABOUT THE AUTHOR

Dimakatso is an author living in Berkshire, England with her husband and four daughters. She was born and bred in Pretoria, South Africa and has degrees in medical sciences from Durban and the U.K. Her mother is Tswana of the Bakgatla tribe and her father is Pedi from whom she developed her love for the Sotho language.